Poets and the Algerian War

edited by Francis Combes
translated by Alan Dent

Smokestack Books
1 Lake Terrace, Grewelthorpe, Ripon HG4 3BU
e-mail: info@smokestack-books.co.uk
www.smokestack-books.co.uk

The copyright of the poems
rests with the authors.

Introduction,
copyright Francis Combes, 2012.

Translation,
copyright Alan Dent 2017.

First published as
Les poètes et la guerre d'Algerie
(Biennale Internationale des Poètes
en Val-de-Marne, 2012)

ISBN 978-0-9955635-3-7

Smokestack Books is represented
by Inpress Ltd

Table de matières

Les poètes et la Guerre d'Algerie, par Francis Combes   11

Les poètes français contre la Guerre d'Algérie
Jaques Dubois, Afrique du Nord 1952   20
Alain Guérin, Mohamed et Jean   28
Madeleine Riffaud, On les tue par le feu, l'eau, l'électricité   36
Madeleine Riffaud, Chanson pour Mouloud   38
Aragon, Le Roman inachevé (extrait)   40
Maurice Cury, Pour la paix   42
Henri Deluy, Paix en Algérie   44
Franck Venaille, Versailles, peut-être   46
Jacques Gaucheron, Cette terre est sa terre   50
Gabriel Cousin, Henri Alleg chez nous en France   54
Bernard Mazo, L'innocence perdue   56
Guillevic, Visages   58
Lanza del Vasto, Non-violence et vérité   60
Pierre Seghers, La gloire   64

Hommage à Maurice Audin
Andrée Barret, Je sais que tes amis te cherchent   68
Gabriel Cousin, La femme de Maurice Audin regarde le silence   70
Henri Deluy, Mens enfants n'ont pas l'âge de raison   72
Jo Guglielmi, Celui qui prend la garde dans nos rêves   74
André Liberati, Celui qui donne au bien son âme   76
Henri Merlen, Audin, jamais plus les campanules ne sonneront   78
Jean Pérol, L'ordre   80
Jean Perret, Mon poème est un hurlement.   82
Charles Dobzynski, Chaque mort avait son visage…   84
Oliven Sten, Poème pour les chiens Kabyles   86
Jo Guglielmi, Algérie interdite   90
Jean-Jacques Viton, Les faits   92
Alain Lance, Toute la nuit   96
Jean Pérol, Dit sans poésie de la colère   98

Contents

Francis Combes, Introduction: Poets and the Algerian War	11

French Poets against the War
Jacques Dubois, North Africa 1952	21
Alain Guérin, Mohamed and Jean	29
Madeleine Riffaud, 'They kill them with fire, water, electricity'	37
Madeleine Riffaud, Song for Mouloud	39
Aragon, *from* The Unfinished Novel	41
Maurice Cury, For Peace	43
Henry Deluy, Peace in Algeria	45
Franck Venaille, Versailles, Perhaps	47
Jacques Gaucheron, This Earth is Her Earth	51
Gabriel Cousin, Henry Alleg at Home in France	55
Bernard Mazo, Lost Innocence	57
Guillevic, Faces	59
Lanza del Vasto, Non-violence and Truth	61
Pierre Seghers, Glory	65

Homage to Maurice Audin
Andrée Barret, 'I know your friends look for you'	69
Gabriel Cousin, 'Maurice Audin's wife looks at the silence'	71
Henri Deluy, 'My children haven't come of age'	73
Jo Guglielmi, 'The one who stands guard in our dreams'	75
André Liberati, 'He who gives himself to good'	77
Henri Merlen, 'Audin, never again will the campanulas ring'	79
Jean Pérol, Order	81
Jean Perret, 'My poem is a howl'	83
Charles Dobzynski, 'Each death had its face'	85
Oliven Sten, Poem for the Dogs of Kabylie	87
Jo Guglielmi, Forbidden Algeria	91
Jean-Jacques Viton, The Facts	93
Alain Lance, 'All night'	97
Jean Pérol, Said Without Poetic Anger	99

Antoine Vitez, Lettre après plus de quatre ans	100
Yves Broussard, Algérie 60	102
G.-L. Godeau, L'encre rouge	104
Henri Meschonnic, Par le fer et le feu	106
Henri Mechonnic, Pour voir clair	108

Poètes algériens et guerre de libération

Noureddine Aba, Mon frère	112
Jean El Mouhoub Amrouche, Le combat algérien	116
Djamal Amrani, Sous un tas de décombres	118
Messaour Boulanouar, J'écris pour que la vie soit respectée par tous	122
Annie Steiner, Ce matin, ils ont osé	126
Mohammed Dib, Sur la terre, errante	128
Anna Gréki, Captif	132
Jean Sénac, Matinale de mon peuple	136
Kateb Yacine, Poussières de juillet	138
Henri Kréa, Lettre à un étranger incompréhensible	144
Nourredine Tidafi, La patrie totale	146
Jean Pélegri, Les paroles de la rose	152
Malek Haddad, Le droit de dire au monde	158
Malek Haddad, Et la paix revenue	160
Bachir Hadj Ali, Serment	162

Poèmes algériens traduits de l'arabe

Omar El Bernaoui, Fierté	166
Mohamed Saleh Baouiya, Le révolutionnaire	168

Poèmes populaires algériens

Un poème kabyle	174
Bwaqel	176

Antoine Vitez, Letter after More than Four Years	101
Yves Broussard, Algeria 60	103
G.-L. Godeau, Red Ink	105
Henri Meschonnic, By Iron and Fire	107
Henri Meschonnic, To See Clearly	109

Algerian poets and the war of liberation

Noureddine Aba, 'My brother'	113
Jean El Mouhoub Amrouche, The Algerian Struggle	117
Djamal Amrani, Under a Pile of Rubble	119
Messaour Boulanouar, 'I write so that life can be respected by all'	123
Annie Steiner, This Morning They Dared	127
Mohammed Dib, On the Earth, Wandering	129
Anna Gréki, Captive	133
Jean Sénac, Morning for My People	137
Kateb Yacine, Dust of July	139
Henri Kréa, Letter to an Incomprehensible Stranger	145
Nourredine Tidafi, The Complete Homeland	147
Jean Pélegri, The Words of the Rose	153
Malek Haddad, The Right to Tell the World	159
Malek Haddad, 'And peace returned'	161
Bachir Hadj Ali, Vow	163

Algerian poems translated from Arabic

Omar El Bernaoui, Pride	167
Mohamed Saleh Baouiya, The Revolutionary	169

Popular Algerian poems

A Poem from Kabylie	175
Bwaqel	177
The Poets	186
Acknowledgements	193

Introduction: Poets and the Algerian War

In *Love at War*, a lecture on poetry and resistance delivered in London in 1945, Paul Eluard said, 'I know that poets have always been thought of as unhappy men. What is often forgotten is that they are unhappy *for* others and not *because* of others. They feel pain for others. Their broken hearts, their loneliness, their defencelessness but also their hope, symbolise the despondency and hope of all men in an imperfect world.'

He added, 'the poet must go to the extreme limit of expression, must have the courage to speak for the mass that keeps quiet,' evoking Baudelaire ('the poet enjoys the incomparable privilege that he can, at will, be himself or someone else'), Nerval ('the life of a poet is that of everyone') and obviously Rimbaud ('I am the other')'.

During the Occupation, events led many poets to try to speak to and for everyone, at a time when the conditions of publication and distribution were more difficult than ever. Suddenly, the Surrealist magic tricks with the marvellous seemed out of place, notwithstanding the fact that some of those who had been through this school remained deeply marked by the freeing of the imagination, even in their more directly political writing.

Although the results were uneven, the Resistance poets tried to renew the link with that enduring capacity of poets to speak for the sufferings of all. Which is why, in Eluard's view, this rediscovered power of poetry seemed to define its very *raison d'être*.

'Put to the test, 'he wrote in conclusion, 'poetry has proved, during these four years, that it is one with the love of liberty. Tomorrow, it will be one, for all men, with the love of life.'

Enough has been written in favour of (and sometime against) Resistance poetry for everyone to know it was a chapter, and perhaps not one of the least, in our literary history. (Consider the achievement of Pierre Seghers and Jacques Gaucheron, or more recently, the anthology *Cent poemes de la resistance* put together by poet and historian Alain Guérin.) But if the example of poets' commitment to the fight against Nazism is well known, their effort to combat colonial wars is less so. However, it was real.

Certainly, in the nineteenth (and at the beginning of the twentieth) century there was no shortage of works which found in 'our colonies 'not only the opportunity for a bit of warlike crowing (these were the least notable poems), but also a new territory, exotic and full of phantasms, which allowed for flights of inspiration. There was always a contradiction about this romanticised Orientalism, because it was simultaneously a curiosity about and an attraction to the foreign, an effort to discover the other, his culture and civilisation, and a tendency stamped with racist prejudices. One of the few to protest against colonialism was Victor Hugo who stood up, in particular, against the attack by French troops on the summer palace in Beijing.

But it was above all at the start of the twentieth century that a real movement of conscience established itself among writers and poets. The Dadaists and Surrealists were certainly among the first. Aragon tells how the Rif war and the massacres of Moroccans engendered in him a sense of dislocation. It played a big role in bringing together those young writers, revolted by the butchery of the First World War, and the intellectuals of the *Clarté* group around Henri Barbusse. The Surrealists called a boycott of the Colonial Exhibition and organised, with others, and exhibition in the *Place du Combat* (today the *Place du colonel Fabien*).

During the Algerian War, reference is often made to the Appeal of the 121, to the role of Jean-Paul Sartre and the review *Les Temps Modernes*, the stand taken by some Christian intellectuals, the action of the 'suitcase carriers' (a French network offering direct help to the FLN), and of course the conscientious objectors who ran the risk of prison.

In fact, the campaign against this war (which the ruling elites insisted on downplaying, with the usual understatement, as 'events'), was various and progressive. It affected all sections of society, the working class as much as intellectuals, and it took many forms. And it included poets.

No doubt their voices did not resonate in France as much some witnesses did – Henri Alleg, for example, who in *La Question* denounced the torture and executions carried out by the French army. But it played its part in the general movement which helped to shift French public opinion.

The poems in this anthology were published in Aragon's *Les Lettres Françaises*, the review *Europe* run by Pierre Abraham and Pierre Gamarra, in pamphlets published by Editeurs Français Réunis and in the recently established review, also based in Marseille, *Action Politique*.

Henri Deluy explains how colonial wars and the independence movements determined the political and social conscience of men and women of his generation – the repression in Madagascar, the war in Indochina, the independence of Tunisia, and then Algeria…

The young poets gathered around *Action Poétique* thought that poetry could and should contribute to changing the world. This struggle against the Algerian War played a large role in their thinking and acting. They took part in demonstrations on the Canebière, attended meetings, in some cases put up flyposters or scrawled slogans on walls. This was at a time when censorship of those opposed to the war was usual under all the various governments of the Fifth Republic.

In 1960, the review published a special anti-Algerian War issue, which sold more than 6,000 copies (as many as the Chile special of 1971) – quite something for a poetry review, even during the 1960s. The range of the writers brought together in this special number was as notable as the variety of their writings and aesthetic positions. Some like Alain Lance, Charles Dobzynski, Franck Venaille and Jo Guglielmi had figured regularly in the review during the 1960s. But there were some less expected guest writers like Eugène Guillevic, Pierre Seghers and Lanza del Vasto. The opinions of the contributors regarding the causes of the war and its solutions were not necessarily identical. Nor were their ideas about poetry.

Les Lettres Françaises regularly published articles and poems about the war. They also published a special number in homage to the Algerian writer Mouloud Feraoun and his companions, who were assassinated by the OAS in El Bia in 1962.

Among the works directly inspired by the war and which have left their mark on French literature, we must of course mention *The Screens* by Jean Genet (1960) and *Tomb for a hundred thousand soldiers* by Pierre Guyotat (turned down by Seuil and published by

Gallimard in 1967). As well as the extract from *Unfinished Novel* published here, which has clear echoes of Algeria, we know also that the war led Aragon to launch himself into a great endeavour of rediscovery of Arab-Andalusian culture, which produced the astonishing book *Mad For Elsa*, at once a huge love poem, a homage to a past civilization and an attempt to open a dialogue between the West and the East....

There are poems in this volume which will stand the test of time. And there are some rediscoveries to be made (for example, Oliven Sten, a poet forgotten today who was once published by Pierre-Jean Oswald.) And there are, no doubt, some not quite so successful poems. But even these interest me for their value as testimony. They remind us that poets did not remain silent. And sometimes, they say much more.

They tell us, for example, that from the beginning of the war, French poets stood up against torture. Such was the case with Madeleine Riffaud, in a poem from September 1955, which is included here and shows no lack of power. Madeleine Riffaud came from the Resistance. She had been tortured and condemned to death by the Germans. During the Algerian War she was a major correspondent for *L'Humanité* and was once more condemned to death, this time by the OAS who made an attempt on her life in a street in Oran.

And as early as 1952 (that is before the outbreak of the war) some people were talking about independence (an idea that wasn't then widespread even among progressives), such as the poet Jacques Dubois in his great reportage poem 'In North Africa' (published by Cercle d'Art and illustrated by Boris Tazlistky and Mireille Miaille. Poets are sometimes groundbreakers (although not that often).

Sometimes a word or image can surprise us, such as 'the Stalinist sun' of Alain Guérin or the 'Lenin' of Jean Perret. But we have to orientate ourselves to the context of the time.

From the Algerian point of view (since this collection brings together French and Algerian poets who wrote during this period) the stakes were not the same. It was a matter not simply of denouncing war, violence and the injustice carried out by the coloniser and its army, but also of affirming a new voice: that of the people demanding its independence. No doubt the poets had a greater impact on that side of the Mediterranean than this (in spite of the illiteracy prevalent among the Algerian population at the time). They were, whether you like it or not, the voice of the new Algeria.

The revolutionary Algerian poetry of these years (represented here by Jean Sénac, Mohamed Dib, Kateb Yacine, Bachir Hadj Ali and others less well-known) bears the hallmark of a new culture, of a country proud of its conquered freedom, of a new relationship between the people and the intellectuals. What would become of it after is another matter. But the vicissitudes of independence (no doubt partly inscribed in the conditions of national liberation) could not justify a return to neo-colonialism or that we should go back on the right of a people to decide their own history.

Most of the Algerian poems from this period are written in French. Hardly surprising. The Arabic alphabet was introduced only late into the school system in Algeria. The few Algerian intellectuals who wrote in Arabic were those who had attended the Arabic university of Zitourna in Tunisia. And, curiously, these aren't the ones who speak most about the war and the Algerian Revolution. But it seemed important to us that some should appear here. In the same way, we've included a poem in the Berber language, whose vitality (especially in song) needs no proof. The few poems by women, translated by Jean Sénac, which bring this collection to a conclusion give an idea of the quality of this popular poetry in Kabyle or Arabic dialect (and will suffice to prove, if in any doubt, that such poetry exists).

Beyond the value as historical documents of these French and Algerian poems, they are of interest because of what they tell us about the relations at once inevitable and difficult that the poem can maintain with historical circumstances in the making.

In 2012 the International Biennial of Poets in the Val-de-Marne decided to open a workshop on this theme: 'Writing the Event'. This publication was one of the contributions to this theme.

The relationship between 'poetry and the event' has used up plenty of ink. Usually to deny that a poem has any relation to its circumstances – from the demand for a pure poetry by Théophile Gautier to Benjamin Péret's pamphlet (*The Poets' Dishonour*) by way of the rejection of 'universal reportage' of Stéphane Mallarmé. But also to defend the insertion of the poet in History – from Goethe writing that all his poems were rooted in circumstance to Mayakovsky looking to define social control in order to pick out those social issues which called for a specifically poetic treatment.

Mayakovsky (who knew political poetry thoroughly) drew attention to an essential problem: the difficulty created by the lack of retreat. And he explained in his essay *How Verses are Made* the means by which the poet we would call 'committed' can compensate for this fault, which is often fatal to the poem. The poetic theorist Predrag Matvejvic later addressed this huge and thorny topic of socially rooted poetry in a vital work of the 1970s, *The Poetry of History*.

The poems collected here (and there are of course absences) show how French and Algerian poets in the 1950s and 1960s were able to write about political events. Not only how these events influenced them, but also how they poetically transformed the primary matter provided them by history in the making. Among some of them can perhaps be discerned the influence of Eluard. Although he died in 1952, two years before the war began, he published in 1948, his collection *Political Poems*).

When you read these poems you see how some poets, faced with historical events, gave full rein to their emotions. Sometimes to their indignation (which according to Juvenal, is part of the great tradition of satirical poetry). You will see too how others grant greater importance to critical reason, to the enunciation of contradictions, even humour and irony; another means of satire. Sometimes the text is this side of events, in tune with them, sometimes ahead.

Why should this be of interest to us today?

The question is pertinent.

Looking at the poetic evolution that the authors brought together in these pages, one cannot but be struck by the fact that for the most part, they have changed a lot. For many, political urgency and poetic interventionism have given way to more formal preoccupations, for example, relating to linguistics or psychoanalysis. Thus, the writing of one or another of them has been transformed. Those who established a certain poetic modernity in the 1970s, are now less concerned with changing the world through poetry, with 'lived poetry' than with the poem defined as a 'work of writing'.

And yet... The period of colonial wars is perhaps nothing more than a page to be turned in the book of history. The iron age of violence for world domination is, unfortunately, not over. From Afghanistan to Libya or Syria, wars are part of our reality. Racism and colonialism too. There are therefore always, here and there, those who are at war with war.

Francis Combes

**French Poets
against the War**

Jacques Dubois

Afrique du Nord 1952

       I

L'aube comme un cheval
Se mit sur les genoux
Devant nous
        Alger se leva

L'Afrique à sa fenêtre
Nous regardait entrer
Je ne venais pas comme un frère

J'étais en uniforme
Et je souffrais de l'être
Trâinant tel un énorme
            paquetage
Mon coeur
Je ne venais pas comme un frère,
Afrique du Nord,
Et tu t'étonnais
         de me voir sans haine
Et tu t'étonnais de me voir sonore

Je ne venais pas comme un frère
Mais je t'aimais sans te connaître
J'étais armé j'étais fermé
J'aurais voulu tendre les bras

Puis j'ai couru tel un insecte
Sur ta colonne vertébrale
J'ai traversé tes paysages
Dans un wagon de marchandises
Comme une valise en transit

Jacques Dubois

North Africa 1952

   I

The dawn like a horse
Went down on its knees
In front of us
    Algiers arose

Africa at its window
Watched us enter
I didn't come as a brother

I was in uniform
And I suffered accordingly
Dragging like an enormous
       package
My heart
I didn't come as a brother,
North Africa
And you were amazed
       to see me without hate
And you were amazed to see me resonant

I didn't come as a brother
But I loved you without knowing you
I was armed I was buttoned up
I would have liked to hold out my arms

Then I ran like an insect
Along your spine
I crossed your landscape
In a freight wagon
Like a suitcase in transit

Je ne venais pas comme un frère
                ô Maghreb
Mais c'est avec tendresse
                que je te découvrais
Comme un chien mal dressé
Je tirais sur ma chaîne
Et je ne venais pas lécher les mains du maître

I didn't come like a brother
                          O Mahgreb
But it was with tenderness
                      I discovered you
Like a badly-trained dog
I strained at my chain
And I didn't come to lick the hands of my master

II

Penché sur les essieux chanteurs
Je regardais passer les villes
J'allais du Sous en Kabylie
Et de Souk-Ahras à Mateur

Le temps commençait à l'Hégire
Je mangeais des beignets au miel
On écorçait les chênes-lièges
Qui ressemblaient à l'Algérie

La conscience en état de siège
Je ne savais comment agir
J'entendais les sergents rugir
En comptant les jours pris au piège

Je ne me croyais pas chez moi
Et mon fusil me faisait honte
Je cueillais du matin au soir
De grandes roses coléreuses
La misère me pesait lourd
Et mon coeur était labourable

II

Leaning on the singing axels
I watched towns pass
I went from the Sous in Kabylie
And from Souk-Arhas to Mateur

Time began at Hegire
I ate doughnuts with honey
We peeled cork-oaks
Which looked like Algeria

My conscience under siege
I didn't know how to act
I heard sergeants bellow
As I counted the days caught in the trap

I didn't feel I was at home
And I was ashamed of my rifle
From morning till evening
I gathered big angry roses
Misery weighed me down
And my heart was arable earth

XXI

La source chante sous la roche
Le jour viendra le jour est proche
Ô Maghreb
Où l'éclair zébrera les ténèbres du bagne
Où le torrent balaiera les montagnes
Où la police
        comptera ses vertèbres
Et les fossiles
        retourneront sous terre

Une immense armée de pieds nus
Monte à l'assaut de la chaussure

Le temps est venu d'embrasser
Avec les lèvres des blessures

Ramdane Bédri
        mon frère
C'est pour toi que j'écris
        que je crie ce poème
J'élève à ta colère cette statue de sel

Vois le passé qui témoigne
De tes lumières poignardées

Voici les justiciers
        à mémoire de pierre
Des soleils inouïs naissent dans la poussière
Le ciel est sous tes pieds

J'écris d'un siècle déchirant
J'écris d'un monde criminel
Et ma page est tachée de sang
J'écris d'un monde qui chancelle`

J'écris d'un monde renaissant
        je chante
L'indépendance de l'Afrique
        je chante
L'épanouissement énorme des patries

XXI

The spring sings beneath the rock
Day will come day is near
Oh Mahgreb
Where lightning will zigzag the prison shadows
Where the torrent will bathe the mountains
Where the police
          will count its vertebrae
And the fossils
          will go back underground

An immense army of bare feet
Mounts an assault on the shoe

The time has come
To kiss the wounds with our lips

Ramdane Bédri
          my brother
It's for you I write
          that I shout this poem
I raise this statue of salt to your anger

See the past which testifies
To your stabbed lights

Here are the lovers of justice
          with memories of stone
Unknown suns are born in the dust
The sun is beneath your feet

I write of a harrowing century
I write of a criminal world
And my page is stained with blood
I write of a collapsing world

I write of a world being reborn
          I sing
The independence of Africa
          I sing
Of the huge blossoming of homelands

Alain Guérin

Mohamed et Jean

Le ciel se froisse sur Paris, comme un mouchoir;
Le jour quitta les rues, quand un flic a tiré.
Il pleuvait, lentement, place de Stalingrad,
Mais la pluie n'était rien, sous le soleil des cris,
Il pleuvait lentement quand un flic a tiré,
Quand Hocine a pâli, quand Hocine est tombé.

En ce soir de victoire, il nous faut regarder,
Droit dans les yeux, le sang; tout le sang répandu,
Le sang, le sang, le sang ne nous rend pas aveugles,
Car l'homme de demain dépasse l'épouvante;
Et le froid peut entrer, frère, sous la peau brune,
Dans ton cœur victorieux la vie chante toujours:
Le défi à la mort illumine nos hymnes!
Un camarade est mort. Tremblez dogues-ministres
Gardes-chiourme engraissés par la chair que calcine
Le napalm inondant de feu le Viet-Nam libre!
Tremblez robots-bourreaux! Vous qui tintez si bien,
Quand dans vos têtes-tronc, le Yankee met sa pièce.
Le meurtre restera. Poings, souvenirs et larmes.
Nul n'oubliera jamais. Assassins vous paierez,
Vous paierez la pâleur d'Hocine assassiné,
La neige rouge aux lèvres, les yeux retournés,
Les sanglots des enfants… Canailles! vous paierez.
Le caillot de son cœur tâchera votre ciel.
Le poids de son corps froid écrasera vos rêves.

Alain Guérin

Mohamed and Jean

The sky crumples like a handkerchief over Paris;
Day was leaving the streets, when a cop fired.
It was raining, slowly, on Stalingrad Square,
But the rain was nothing, beneath the sun of cries,
It was raining slowly when a cop fired,
When Hocine went pale, when Hocine fell.

On this evening of victory, we must look
Blood full in the eyes; all the spilled blood,
Blood, blood, blood doesn't make us blind,
Because tomorrow's man goes beyond terror;
And cold can enter, brother, under brown skin,
In your victorious heart life still sings:
The defiance of death brightens our hymns!
A comrade is dead. Tremble watchdog ministers
Galley-masters fattened by roasted flesh
Napalm flooding with fire free Vietnam!
Tremble robot executioners! You who sound so nicely
When the Yankee slips his coin into your wooden heads.
Murder will remain. Fists, memories and tears.
No one will ever forget. You will pay, assassins
You will pay for the pallor of the murdered Hocine.
Red snow around his lips, his eyes upturned
The sobbing of children... Dogs! You will pay.
The pebble of his heart will stain your sky.
The weight of his cold body will crush your dreams.

Terre aux cheveux de feu, dépeignés par le crime,
Monde nocturne pris aux rets des parasites,
Que se taisent soudain les radios d'insomnie
Un prolétaire est mort, abattu par les flics!
De Bougie, de Guelma, d'Oran au Sud brûlé,
Sur leurs couches de fric, de kif et de démence,
Les colons, leurs bouffons, leurs valets et leurs sbires,
Enivrés par le vin qu'à la terre ils imposent,
Suffoqués par l'odeur de la sueur sacrifiée,
Retroussent en gloussant, leurs babines de hyènes.
L'empereur du phosphate et le roi de l'alfa
Volent que l'on pense à eux aux Compteurs de Montrouge.

Le même coffre-fort étouffe nos amours,
Mohamed de Sétif et Jean de Saint-Denis.
On tue un Algérien pour mieux vendre la France.
Ce sang qui fait flamber les pavés sous la pluie,
Nourrit aussi les lueurs du néon de Broadway,
Ta peur féroce de la paix, monde incurable,
Soumet au Dieu Dollar, le Moloch colonial.

Les chômeurs que l'espoir de manger expatrie,
Portent, plaie dans leur chair, la chaîne impérialiste.
Ils sont venus trompés, devenus marchandises;
Le cargo cahotait dans l'écume enchaînée,
Et les os, sous leurs yeux, saillaient, comme l'Aurès
Sous la terre épuisée que gratte en vain leur père.
Ils sont venus trompés, un trafiquant d'espoir,
Achetant pour cent francs une poignée de muscles,
Avait fait miroiter à leurs yeux affamés
Un Paris de pain blanc, une chemise blanche…
La Méditerranée – mourante – les traîna
Jusqu'au quais gangrenés de quelque port de pègre.

Land with hair aflame, ruffled by crime,
Nighttime world caught in the nets of parasites,
Let the insomniac radios fall silent
A worker is dead, shot down by the cops!
From Bougie, from Guelma, from the burnt south of Oran,
On their beds of money, dope and madness,
The colonels, their clowns, their servants and their time-serving policeman
Intoxicated by the wine they force on the earth,
Suffocated by the odour of the sweat of sacrifice,
Pull back, chuckling, their hyena lips.
The emperor of phosphate and the king of alfalfa
See that people think of them behind the counters in Montrouge.

The same safe strangles our love,
Mohamed from Setif and Jean from Saint-Denis.
They kill an Algerian the better to be able to market France.
This blood which makes the paving stones flame beneath the rain,
Also feeds the neon lights of Broadway,
Your ferocious fear of peace, incorrigible world,
Submitted to the Dollar God, the colonial Moloch.

The unemployed exiled by their hope of food,
Carry, as a wound in their flesh, the chain of imperialism.
They arrived deceived, became commodities;
The cargo tossed in the chained foam,
And the bones, under their eyes, stuck out like Atlas
Under the exhausted earth their father scratches in vain.
They arrived deceived, a hope dealer
Buying for a hundred francs a handful of muscles,
Had made their starved eyes reflect
A Paris of white bread, a white shirt…
The Mediterranean – dying – dragged them
To the gangrenous quays of some thieves' port.

Soleil sur les rochers, tournant, fouet minéral,
Astre cravaché, chômage, ignorance,
Eclipse du sang, du rire et de l'air –
Ils t'ont fui mais voilà que la neige nocturne
S'empare de leurs cœurs inconnus et troqués.
Les pavés, aux clartés saccagées par la boue,
Alourdissent la nuit des pauvres gens. Mon frère
A la peau de soleil, Ahmed ou toi, Kadour,
Tu lances vainement tes mots tissés de siècles
Ta phrase où le Simoum lève l'aile des verbes.
Grillage des égouts, tôle des pissotières;
Tout te devient prison, partout un commissaire
Te poursuit; et tu n'as qu'un mètre cube d'air
Pour avoir faim la nuit, rêvant à la fontaine
Où ton plus jeune enfant mire ses yeux rongés,
Rongés par le trachôme, Ahmed, ou toi, Kadour,
Dans la chambre d'hôtel vingt hommes nus s'entassent:
Dix manœuvres le jour, dix manœuvres la nuit.

Sun on the rocks, turning, mineral whip,
Star riding crop, unemployment, ignorance,
Eclipse of blood of laughter of air –
They fled from you but see how the nocturnal snow
Takes hold of their unknown and exchanged hearts.
The paving stones, in light disordered by mud
Weigh down the night of the poor. My brother
Skin of sunshine, Ahmed or you, Kadour,
You launch in vain words woven of centuries
Your phrase in which the Simoum raises the wing of the verbs.
Drain grids, sheet metal of urinals;
Everything becomes your prison, an official
Pursues you everywhere, and you have only a cubic metre of air
To be hungry at night, dreaming of the fountain
Where your youngest child's eaten eyes are mirrored
Eaten by trachoma, Ahmed, or you Kadour,
In the hotel room twenty naked men are piled up:
Ten manoeuvres during the day, ten manoeuvres during the night.

Sous le métro qui geint – comète mécanique –
Jetant dans le canal de pâles poignées d'ombres,
Stalingrad – Jean Jaurès respire étrangement.
Hocine assassiné, la police est partie…
Et de longs groupes d'hommes, parlant à voix basse,
Passent, avec d'immenses drapeaux dans les yeux.
Ahmed et Mohamed sont là – et mille et mille,
De leurs frères unis aux meilleurs de la France.
Hocine n'est pas mort d'une balle perdue!
Et Kadour de Sétif, et Jean-Louis de Saint-Denis,
Les affamés, les avilis, les écrasés,
Par la faim, la douleur, l'injustice, l'opium
Relèvent leur grand front où les rides dessinent
Vos visages, patries qu'on a défigurées!
Des lourds limons du Gange aux sables d'Agadir,
Et à Paris ce soir, l'homme fait sortir l'aube
Des banques où l'avaient enfermée les pillards.
La Bourse baisse, et la folie du bourreau monte,
Quand il sent déferler sur ses tempes de pierre
Un milliard de pieds nus qui brisent leurs entraves,
Un milliard d'yeux mûris au soleil stalinien,
D'yeux fixés sur la lutte du printemps chinois
Où pousse un chrysanthème énorme: le bonheur

1954

Beneath the groaning metro – mechanical comet –
Casting on the canal pale handfuls of shadows,
Stalingrad – Jean Jaurès is breathing strangely.
Hocine assassinated, the police left…
And long groups of men, speaking in low voices
Go by, immense flags in their eyes.
Ahmed and Mohamed are there – and thousands and thousands
Of their brothers united for the best of France.
Hocine didn't die from a stray bullet!
And Kadour from Sétif, and Jean-Louis from Saint-Denis,
The starving, the reviled, the crushed,
By hunger, by pain, by injustice, by opium
Raise their great forehead where the lines depict
Your faces, disfigured homelands!
From the heavy lime of the Ganges to the sands of Agadir,
And in Paris this evening, man brings forth the dawn
Of the banks where the pillagers had imprisoned him.
The Stock Exchange falls, and the madness of the executioner rises,
When he feels unfurling on his stone temples
A million bare feet which break their fetters,
A million eyes ripened in the sun,
Eyes fixed on the struggle of the Chinese spring
Where a huge chrysanthemum grows: happiness!

1954

Madeleine Riffaud

On les tue par le feu, l'eau, l'électricité
Eux qui vécurent loin des sources
Et rêvant d'eau toute leur vie
Eux qui grelottaient, sans charbon
Au soleil glacé du Mouloud.
Eux qui veillaient sans lumière
Au fond d'un bidonville obscur.

La première fois qu'il vit
De près
Une baignoire
Fut le dernier jour de sa vie.

Septembre 1955

Madeleine Riffaud

They kill them with fire, water, electricity
Those who lived far from springs
Dreaming of water all their life
Those who shivered, without coal
In Mouloud's frozen sun.
Those who lay awake in the dark
Buried in a gloomy slum.

The first time he saw
A bath
Close up
Was the last day of his life.

September 1955

Madeleine Riffaud

Chanson pour Mouloud

Mouloud a pris quatre brindilles
Pour se bâtir une maison,
Aux murs de boue, la paille brille,
On peut y loger deux grillons.

Mouloud a cueilli des piquants
Au figuier qui lui sert d'abri.
Un Algérien vieux de quatre ans
Sait qu'il doit défendre sa vie.

Mouloud a orné sa maison
D'un diamant de verre cassé
Si c'est plus beau chez le colon
Moi j'ai l'étoile, au ciel brisée.

Mouloud autour de sa maison
A dressé en rempart, des pierres.
Bien plus solide est la prison
Où ils ont enfermé son père.

Le froid est bleu sous les haillons.
Or les grillons pourront chanter:
Mouloud a bâti sa maison
La première qu'il eût jamais.

Mais le C.R.S. est passé
Casque, fusil et revolver.
D'un seul soulier a écrasé
Les deux grillons, l'étoile en verre.

Madeleine Riffaud

Song for Mouloud

Mouloud took four twigs
To build himself a house,
On the wooden walls, the straw shines
You could house two crickets there.

Mouloud gathered nettle
From the fig tree which shelters him.
A four-year-old Algerian
Knows he has to defend his life.

Mouloud decorated his house
With a diamond of broken glass
If the colonist's country is more beautiful
I have the star from the broken sky.

Mouloud put stones around his house
As a rampart.
The prison where they put his father
Is far more robust..

The cold is blue under rags.
Now the crickets will be able to sing:
Mouloud has built his house
The first he ever had.

But the C.R.S. came by,
Helmet, rifle and revolver.
The first boot crushed
The two crickets, the glass star.

Aragon

Le Roman inachevé (extrait)

Ses cheveux sont frisés Il rêve à l'Algérie
Il fait un carton dans un tir du boulevard
Il s'arrête un instant dans une brasserie
A moins qu'il ne se soit assis dans un Milk-Bar
Pour rouler dans ses doigts la rancune du gris

Ou bien c'est la kermesse et sa tête de laine
S'appuie à l'appareil qu'il écoute debout
Il a pour la musique un attrait de phalène
Pour lui cette chanson semble être un rendez-vous
Ce qu'il aime cet air qui dit Plaine ma plaine

Et dans ses yeux mi-clos se lèvent des palmiers
Le petit âne a la couleur de la colline
Ma mère avait les yeux plus noirs que les ramiers
L'eau petitement coule où la tuile l'incline
Mon enfance revient dans ses pas coutumiers

Plaine ma plaine où toute lumière est si vive
Qu'elle brûle son ombre étroite à l'olivier
Et la vie a le goût et le feu de l'olive
Ô fellahs c'est ce paysage où vous viviez
En ces temps sans expédition punitive

Plaine ma plaine où le nuage est un passant
Plaine sans pluie un jour où tomba la colère
Et depuis ce jour-là dans le village absent
Monte l'odeur du chaume et des chairs qui brûlèrent
Et la terre altérée appelle un autre sang

1956

Aragon

from The Unfinished Novel

His hair is curly He dreams of Algeria
He shoots a little target in the boulevard's gallery
He stops a moment in a brasserie
Unless he's sitting in a Milk-Bar
To roll between his fingers the bitterness of tobacco

Or it's the village fete and his woolly head
Leans on the phone he listens to standing up
He's drawn to music like a moth to a flame
For him this song is like a meeting place
How he loves this tune which says Country my country

And in his half-closed eyes palm trees rise up
The little donkey the same colour as the hill
My mother had eyes as dark as a ring-dove's
Water runs in rivulets where the tile slopes
My childhood returns to its usual round

Country my country where all light is so bright
It burns the narrow shadow of the olive tree
And life has the taste and the fire of the olive
Oh fellaheen this is the landscape where you lived
In those times without punitive expeditions

Country my country where the cloud is a passer-by
Country without rain where one day anger landed
And since that day in the absent village
Rises the odour of thatch and flesh that burnt
And the altered earth calls for another blood

1956

Maurice Cury

Pour la paix

Les rues pleurèrent leur misère
C'était un soir comme autrefois
Nous aurions voulu le bonheur
On nous déguisa en soldat
C'était si peu de nous donner
La paix dans les bouquets de fleurs
Dans les yeux dans les fremmes sereines
Ils nous offrirent des décombres
Et la mort à pleines brassées
Nos tout puissants ministres de la peur
Nos anciens guerriers nostalgiques
Désiraient que nous devinissions
Des tueurs et des tortionnaires
Contre les peuples opprimés
Qui désiraient leur liberté
Nous ne sommes pas des guerriers
Et pour l'amitié des chevaux
Le sourire des enfants pâles
Dans leurs écoles de plein vent
Pour les larmes des femmes mères
Pour le pain et le soleil
Pour que les rues puissant renaître
Derrière leurs façades noires
Nous risquons de vouloir la paix
Contre la loi des assassins
L'amour est traqué sur la Terre
Pourtant ton corps vaut bien qu'on vive
Et je chemine vers ma gloire
Dans le secret de tes genoux.

31 Octobre 1956

Maurice Cury

For Peace

The streets cry their misery
It was an evening like in the old days
We would have liked to be happy
They disguised us as soldiers
It didn't come to much to give us
Peace in bouquets of flowers
In the eyes of serene women
They offered us debris
And armfuls of death
Our all-powerful ministers of fear
Our nostalgic ex-warriors
Wanted us to become
Killers and torturers
Against oppressed people
Who wanted their freedom
We aren't warriors
And for the friendship of horses
The smile of pale children
In their open-air schools
For the tears of mothers
For bread and sunshine
So that the streets could be reborn
Behind their black facades
We risk wanting peace
Against the law of the assassins
Love is stalked across the earth
All the same your body makes life worth living
And I make my way towards my glory
In the secret of your knees.

31 October 1956

Henri Deluy

Paix en Algérie

Cette guerre, j'ai vieilli avec elle
Ces meurtres sont les miens
Ils ont laissé des premiers jours comme un retour de flamme
Où la mort devient une lente blessure
Cette blessure en moi, et toujours le poème sur ce même chemin
Ce même désarroi pour retrouver ma douleur dans ses cris

Je sais et ne sais plus combien d'heures ont
    passé par cette zone d'usure où la parole
    est au mensonge, car ces meurtres sont
    les miens sans l'être tout à fait, ma vie
    continue et j'oublie parfois les enfants
    morts et leurs mères et leurs pères réduits
    sous la cendre

Je sais bien que cette ombre blanche des mélèzes,
    l'autre soir, un instant fut tout pour moi

Je sais aussi et le poème ne peut choisir
Ce que nous savons tous
Et qui barre toute chose jusqu'au bout
C'est pourquoi
Nous pour qui la parole est un acte
Nous avons fait notre choix parmi les mots
Parmi les plus abstraits
Les plus difficiles

Ensemble nous avons mis la Paix dans nos projets d'avenir
Au devant de la porte
Ensemble nous avons mis la Paix dans l'immédiat

Dans l'armoire quotidienne
Avec le linge des enfants.

Henry Deluy

Peace in Algeria

This war, I've grown old with it
These murders are mine
They've left, as it were, from the first days a back-firing
Where death becomes a slow wound
This wound in me, and always the poem on this same path
This same disarray on finding my pain in its cries

I know and no longer know how many hours have
    passed in this arena of usury where speech
    is lying, because these murders are
    mine without being completely mine, my life
    goes on and sometimes I forget the dead
    children and their mothers and fathers lying
    under ash

I know well that this white shadow of the larch
    the other evening was for a moment everything for me

I know too the poem can't choose
What we all know
And which stands in the way of everything forever
That's why
We for whom speech is an act
We have made our choice among words
Among the most abstract
The most difficult

Together we have put Peace in our plans for the future
Before the door
Together we have put Peace in the immediate

In the everyday cupboard
With the children's underwear.

Franck Venaille

Versailles, peut-être

Dans le parc où le soleil rendait les pavés en poussière les jardins à la française et cette envie irraisonnée de t'embrasser tous les mètres tu étais ce que j'avais de meilleur au monde avec ta robe que je connais par cœur ta peau tellement bronzée que t'avoir dans mes bras c'était être couché sur le sable le marché rue Vaugirard quand j'avais ta main et plus tard sur un banc tes lèvres après ces jours à avoir si faim

> Les caisses sont là mon lieutenant et c'était impossible de ne pas avoir la gorge serrée dans ce train qui roule à vingt-cinq à l'heure il y a en a un sur trois qui déraille et les caisses sont là destination Souk Ahras vingt-huit morts et quatre prisonniers à Mondovi là-bas sa maison est entourée de barbelés mais qui comprend l'Envers et l'Endroit ici j'ai l'impression d'être en plein bagne et c'est parce que tu m'écris mon chéri que j'ai envie de partir te retrouver tu ne peux pas savoir comme j'ai besoin de toi

Il arrive au moins trente paras blessés avec celui qui se tient le ventre c'est sûrement le commando qui est harcelé et nos G.M.C. tournent déjà dans la cour de qui ai-je l'air avec ce P.M. dont je ne voulais pas me servir et la nuit sous les couvertures j'ai froid et j'ai chaud je rêve de ton corps mais pas loin de moi les prisonniers hurlent à cause de la magnéto qu'est-ce que cela veut dire de vivre sans toi à se rabâcher toujours la même chose ma tête dans tes cheveux je m'en moquais bien de l'Algérie avec ses boîtes de ration et le premier qui ramène la vérole du B.M.C dit le capitaine

Franck Venaille

Versailles, Perhaps

In the park where the sun made the flagstones dusty the gardens typically French and me wanting unreasonably to kiss you every metre you were the best thing I had in the world your dress that I knew by heart your skin so tanned that having you in my arms was to be lying on the sand in the Vaugirard Street market when I held your hand and later on a bench your lips after those days of such hunger

> The crates are here my lieutenant and it was impossible not to have a parched throat in this train running at twenty-five kilometres an hour one in three comes off the rails and the crates are there destination Souk Ahras twenty-eight dead and four prisoners in Mondovi there her house is surrounded by barbed wire but who can understand Betwixt and Between here I have the feeling of being in a prison and it's because you write to me sweetheart that I want to set off to met you you can't imagine how much I need you

At least thirty paratroops injured including the one who's clutching his stomach the commando is certainly under pressure and our GMC are already turning in the yard of what-do-I-look-like with this training session I didn't want to make use of and at night beneath the covers I'm cold and I'm hot and I dream of your body but not far from me the prisoners are shouting because of the magneto what does it mean to live without you to keep repeating the same things to myself my head in your hair I didn't care a fig for Algeria with its ration boxes and the first who comes back with syphilis from the field brothel says the captain

A part cela ils étaient quatre pour tenir la fille pendant que l'autre la violait est-ce que tu as toujours tes mêmes yeux et la rue de Seine et les quais les gourbis qui flambent là-bas ce poulet déjà raide qui n'entre pas dans ma poche j'ai faim j'ai soif de toi de jour en jour plus envie de toi rien que de toi comme au parc avec ta robe mais ce sang qui reste collé au treillis six mois sans toucher à une femme ce sera toi ou rien que ton ombre que tes lèvres qui me tiennent éveillé pendant le quart la sentinelle de la deux a vu des lumières rien que toi rien que cet amour plus violent plus âpre que la nuit qui nous entoure.

1958

Apart from that there were four of them holding the girl while the others raped her do you still have the same eyes at Seine Street and the quays the burning huts over there this stiff chicken which won't go in my pocket I'm hungry I'm thirsty for you day by day want you more nothing but you as in the park with your dress but this blood which remains stuck to the trellis six months without touching a woman it will be you or nothing your shadow your lips which keep me awake during the watch the two o'clock sentry has seen lights nothing but you nothing but this love more violent more bitter than the night around us

1958

Jacques Gaucheron

Cette terre est sa terre

Le paysage ici soulève à bout de bras
Jusqu'aux confins du ciel
Des montagnes de roc des rochers de soleil

Assise là tout près silencieuse
Leïla d'aube en aube obstinément trieuse
De graines
       Leïla veille écoutant couler
Contre son cœur le sablier de la souffrance

Le sombre des buissons là-bas frissonne
Quelque chose a bougé une forme s'avance
Il vient de loin et c'est un homme
N'en doutez pas

Il vient comme un berger du fond des âges
Il fait un pas
           et puis un pas
Après un autre comme s'il dénouait
Maille après maille quelque chaîne
Sur cette terre
Et c'est sa terre
C'est la sienne

Quand il aura passé ce terrain de pierraille
Quand il sera devant
Qu'on le verra soudain plus grand
Que les montagnes dont il descend
Quand il aura souri dans les yeux clairs de Leïla
Il sourira elle sourira
N'en doutez pas

Alors il n'y aura plus d'ombre en Algérie
Que celle du soleil et c'est une ombre amie

Jacques Gaucheron

This Earth is Her Earth

The landscape here rises at arm's length
To the sky's limits
Mountains of rock rocks of sun

Sitting here close by silent
Leïla from dawn to dawn obstinate sifter
Of grain
      Leïla watches listening to the flow
Against her heart of the egg-timer of suffering

Over there the shadows of the bushes shiver
Something has moved a form comes forward
It comes from far away and it's a man
Have no doubt

He comes like a shepherd from the depth of the ages
He takes a step
              and then one step
After another as if he were unpicking
Link by link some chain
On this earth
And it's her earth
It's hers

When he's passed over this stony terrain
When he's before her
When he will suddenly look bigger
Than the mountains he came down from
When he smiles into the Leïla's clear eyes
He will smile she will smile
Have no doubt

Then there will be no more shadows in Algeria
Other than the sun's and that's a friendly shadow

Sa terre le fait naître
Son pas le fait grandir

Déjà et pour toujours
Il marche sur sa terre

Déjà
N'en doutez pas.

Avril 1958

Her earth gives birth to him
Her step makes him grow

Already and for always
He walks on the earth

Already
Have no doubt

April 1958

Gabriel Cousin

Henri Alleg chez nous en France

Dans Lille la travailleuse il y a un beffroi
tout neuf et les habitants sont très propres.
Dans la cave on a installé une baignoire pour baigner
    Les Arabes.

Dans Strasbourg, il y a une cathédrale
toute en dentelle et les habitants sont gais.
Dans son ombre, se dresse une planche
avec des cordes pour faire rire
    Les « Bicots ».

Dans Lyon, il y a deux fleuves qui font l'amour
et les habitants aiment le boire et le bon manger.
Derrière certains murs il y a des brocs d'eau
et des entonnoirs pour donner à boire
    Aux « Crouillats ».

Dans Marseille passe le mistral aux poumons
purs et les habitants regardent la mer.
Dans une ville face au large des hommes
regardent leur bourreau. Ce sont
    Des « Fellagas ».

Dans Versailles les touristes viennent
en rangs admirer le château du Roi-Soleil
et le soir l'électricité berce la ville de son
    et lumière.

Dans un commissariat près du parc automnal,
les électrodes sont appliquées sur un homme
dont le corps s'emplit de cris et d'éblouissements.
    Il est Algérien.

Les policiers pour couvrir ses cris branchent
le poste de radio qui fait entendre la voix de
Monsieur André Malraux :

    « J'affirme que la torture a cessé en Algérie ».

Gabriel Cousin

Henry Alleg at Home en France

In hard-working Lille there's a belfry
quite new and the inhabitants are very clean
In the cellar they've installed a bath to bathe
    the Arabs.

In Strasbourg, there's a cathedral all
draped in lace and the inhabitants are gay.
In its shadow, rises a plank with
ropes to give a laugh to
    the 'niggers'.

In Lyon, there are two rivers which
make love and the inhabitants like to drink and eat well.
Behind certain walls there are jugs of water
and funnels for people to drink from
    In the 'Crouillats'

In Marseille blows the pure-lunged mistral
and the inhabitants watch the sea.
In a town facing the open water men watch
their executioner. They are
    the 'bandits'.

In Versailles the tourists come in
hordes to admire the palace of the Sun King and
in the evening the electricity nurses the city
    in its light.

In a police station near the autumnal
park, electrodes are placed on a
man whose body fills with cries and dizziness.
    He is Algerian.

To muffle his cries the policemen
turn on the radio which brings the voice
of Monsieur André Malraux:

'I assert that torture has stopped in Algeria.'

Bernard Mazo

L'innocence perdue

Jadis, en ce pays de figuiers et de pierre ocre
Les visages épousaient la configuration secrète
De très anciennes civilisations
L'homme n'était pas ici debout pour défier l'univers
Et dans le vent chaud des Aurès le soleil
Lui prêtait d'éclatantes certitudes
Tandis que les femmes de la tribu inlassablement
Tissaient leurs rêves en forme d'amphores
Ici jadis l'argile des mechtas au surplomb des djebels
Suffisait à conjurer l'épervier de la mort.

Mais aujourd'hui sur cette terre martyrisée
Où la flûte des montagnes s'est tue
Tout se fend maintenant
Par la force des choses
Tout se délivre
Par la force des fusils
Tout se déchire
Par la force des cris
Mais à la fin
Combien seront-ils debout encore
droits dans le soleil à survivre
Combien seront-ils à défier l'éclat meurtrier des armes?

Aurès, Algérie 1959

Bernard Mazo

Lost Innocence

Formerly, in this land of fig-trees and yellow stone
Faces were wedded to the secret configuration
Of very ancient civilizations
Man here didn't stand upright to defy the universe
And in the warm wind of Aurès the sun
Lent him dazzling certainties
While the women of the tribe tirelessly
Wove their dreams into the shape of amphora
Here formerly the clay of the villages on the mountain's overhang
Was enough to summon the sparrow-hawk of death.

But today in this martyred land
Where the summit of the mountains has fallen silent
Everything splits now
By the force of circumstance
Everything is got rid of
By the power of rifles
Everything tears itself
By the power of cries
But finally
How many will still be standing
surviving upright in the sun
How many will defy the murderous brilliance of weaponry?

Aurès, Algeria 1959

Guillevic

Visages

Meurent dans des collines
Que je ne connais guère
Des hommes de chez nous
Que je n'ai pas connus.

Meurent dans des collines
Que je ne connais guère
Des hommes d'Algérie
Que je ne connais pas.

Que je connais peut-être
A travers d'autres hommes
Que je connais un peu
Et je les cherche dans ceux-là.

C'est à ceux qu'on rencontre,
A ceux qui ont visage encore,
Qu'on demande pardon
Pour ceux qui n'en ont plus.

Guillevic

Faces

Dying in the hills
That I hardly know
Are men from my home
Who I didn't know.

Dying in the hills
That I hardly know
Are men from Algeria
That I don't know.

That maybe I know
Through other men
Who I know a little
And who I look for in them.

From the ones you meet
The ones who still have a face
You ask forgiveness
On behalf of those who no longer do.

Lanza del Vasto

Non-violence et vérité

Gandhi enseigne que la non-violence et la vérité sont une seule et même chose, le revers et l'avers de la même médaille. En d'autres termes Mensonge et Violence sont la même chose. De quoi la Guerre d'Algérie offre une nouvelle illustration. L'atrocité particulière de cette guerre dépend en effet de deux grands mensonges qui en ont engendré toute une série d'autres. Le premier c'est que « l 'Algérie c'est la France », le second que la Guerre d'Algérie, c'est la pacification.

Heureux les doux dont les yeux enfin virent
Le vieillard sur le seuil de sa hutte
Et connurent leur Roi, et le bénirent.
Mais plus encore ceux qui suivirent
Cette douceur terrible dans la lutte,
Son ordre clair, son sourire et son Nom
Plus forts que la matraque et le canon.

Seul vainqueur de la Force et de l'Empire
Des vieux démons et des dieux d'aujourd'hui
Vainqueur du Trop, de la Hâte et du Bruit,
Du Bureau, de la banque et de la Bourse
Vainqueur de l'Or, vainqueur de la Machine
Vengeur du Bras et Redresseur d'échines,
Vengeur prêchant comme chantent les sources
Bonté de fer droite comme une lame
Soignant celui qui mord, par le pardon,
Au vol, au dol répondant par le nom,
Gandhi, grande âme.

Lanza del Vasto

Non-violence and Truth

Gandhi teaches that non-violence and truth are one and the same, two sides of the same coin. In other words, Lying and Violence are the same thing. Something illustrated anew by the Algerian War. The particular atrocity of this war depends on two great lies which have given rise to whole series of others. The first is that 'Algeria is France', the second is that the Algerian War is a war of pacification.

Happy the gentle souls whose eyes finally saw
The old man on the step of his hut
And recognised their King, and blessed him.
But even more those who followed
This terrible sweetness into the struggle,
His clarity, his smile and his Name
Stronger than the truncheon and the cannon.

Sole vanquisher of Force and Empire
Of the old demons and today's gods
Vanquisher of the Excessive, the Hasty and of Noise,
Of the Office, the bank and the Stock Exchange
Vanquisher of gold, vanquisher of the machine
Avenger of the Arm and Straightener of spines,
Avenger preaching like streams sing
Iron goodness straight as a blade
Caring for he who bites, by forgiveness,
Responding to theft or fraud with the name
Gandhi, great soul.

Vainqueur de la prison et des supplices,
Libre lui seul que nul péché n'enchaîne
Seul assez fort pour supporter la peine
D'un peuple, et pur, pour expier ses vices.
Des parias, vengeur de l'injustice
Que la coutume et les dieux abritèrent,
Seul révolté que nul complot ne tisse
(Mystère de la clarté n'a rien à taire
Et n'eut jamais le secret pour refuge).
Vainqueur des tribunaux, juge des juges
Seul conquérant pur du sang de ses frères.
Vainqueur serein de la gloire et du blâme
Soldat de paix dont la conquête est don
Armé de force et paré de pardon,
Gandhi, grande âme.

Vainqueur du Trône et de l'office,
Régnant par droit divin de sainteté,
Seul homme ayant sur l'homme autorité,
Qui la mesure au poids du sacrifice.
Vainqueur d'amour châtiant ce qu'il aime.
Vainqueur du monde et vainqueur de soi-même.
Vainqueur au cœur ouvert aux mains ouvertes
Dont la victoire est une découverte
Aux continents de l'humaine grandeur.
Simplicité tranchant toutes les trames,
Gloire solaire du rouet, fil de candeur,
Gandhi, grande âme.

Vanquisher of prison and of punishments,
Only he is free who is chained by no sin
The only one strong enough to bear the pain
Of a people, and pure, to expiate its vices.
Avenger of the injustice to pariahs
Hidden by custom and the gods,
The only rebel not enmeshed in plots
(Mystery of the clarity with nothing to hide
And never had secret as a refuge).
Vanquisher of courts, judge of judges
Sole pure conqueror of the blood of his brothers.
Serene vanquisher of glory and of blame
Soldier for peace whose conquest is a gift
Armed with power and ready to pardon,
Gandhi, great soul.

Vanquisher of the throne and of the office,
Reigning by the divine right of sainthood,
Sole man having authority over man,
Measured by the weight of sacrifice.
Vanquisher of love correcting those he loves.
Vanquisher of the world and vanquisher of himself.
Open-hearted, open-armed vanquisher
Whose victory is a discovery
In the continents of human greatness.
Simplicity cutting through all weaves,
Sunny glory of the spinning-wheel, thread of candour
Gandhi, great soul.

Pierre Seghers

La gloire

Mon beau dragon, mon lance-flammes
Mon tueur mon bel assassin
Ma jolie brute pour ces dames
Mon amour mon trancheur de seins
Mon pointeur mon incendiaire
En auras-tu assez brûlé
Des hommes et violé
Des jeunes filles impubères.

Broyeur de mort lanceur de feu
Rôtisseur de petits villages
Mon bel envoyé du Bon Dieu
Mon archange Mon enfant sage
Bardé de cuir casqué de fer
Fusilleur Honneur de la race
Que rien ne repousse où tu passes
Mon soldat Mon fils de l'enfer.

Va dans tes bêtes mécaniques
Ecraser ceux qui sont chez eux
Va de l'Equateur aux Tropiques
Arracher le bonheur des yeux
Va mon fils va tu civilises
Et puis meurs comme à Epinal
Sur une terre jaune et grise
Où nul ne te voulait de mal.

Pierre Seghers

Glory

My beautiful dragon, my flame-thrower
My killer my beautiful assassin
My pretty brute for these ladies
My love my breast slicer
My time-keeper my fire-brand
Will you have burnt enough
Men and raped
Enough pre-pubescent girls?

Death grinder fire thrower
Village burner
My beauty sent by the Good Lord
My archangel My good child
Clad in leather iron helmeted
Rifleman Honour of the race
Let nothing re-grow where you have been
My soldier My son of Hell.

Go amongst your mechanical beasts
To crush people in their homes
Go from the equator to the tropics
Tear happiness from eyes
Go my son go you civilize
And then die as in Épinal
On a yellow and grey earth
Where no one meant you any harm.

Hommage à Maurice Audin

Le onze juin 1957 à Alger, les parachutistes arrêtent Maurice Audin, assistant à la Faculté des Sciences... Le vingt-et-un juin, selon la version officielle, il s'évade. En fait, Maurice Audin a été étranglé, après de longues séances de torture.

Homage to Maurice Audin

On 11 June 1957 in Algiers, the paras arrested Maurice Audin, a teacher in the Faculty of Science. On 21 June, according to the official version, he escaped. In fact, Maurice Audin had been strangled, after being extensively tortured.

Andrée Barret

Je sais que tes amis te cherchent
Pleins de toi leurs gestes quotidiens
Leurs regards quotidiens doivent s'épouvanter
Lorsqu'ils agitent somnambuliques le passé

Mort pour ce qu'ils aimaient le plus au monde mais n'importe
Tu es mort tu leur manques ils ont horreur de l'aube

Pour moi tu n'es pas mort je viens de te connaître
Lorsque je veux parler je me heurte à ta voix
A ton regard lorsque je vois
Ma souffrance tu la mesures sans pitié

Andrée Barret

I know your friends look for you
Their daily gestures are full of your presence
Their daily looks must be terrified
When sleep-walking they stir up the past

Dead for what they loved most in the world but what matter
You are dead they miss you they are horrified by dawn

For me you aren't dead I have just got to know you
When I want to speak I collide with your voice
With your gaze when I see
Pitilessly you measure my suffering

Gabriel Cousin

La femme de Maurice Audin regarde le silence.
Djamila Bouhired écoute le ciel chaque matin
Et vous mon cher collègue?

Oh! Moi, vous savez à Pâques cette année, j'ai choisi la Toscane.
La terre de Sienne n'est pas encore si rouge que cela!

Et vous?

La misère espagnole est si curieuse…

Et vous?

La truite, la truite. Le silence. Les cheveux de l'eau.
Une connaissance lente et fidèle comme pour une femme…

Ah! Quand donc les gens de mon pays…
les braves gens, bien sûr…
recevront-ils la petite semence de l'inquiétude
qui fait lever l'intolérable angoisse de l'injustice.

Gabriel Cousin

Maurice Audin's wife looks at the silence.
Djamila Bouhired listens to the sky each morning
And you my dear colleague?

Oh! me, you know at Easter this year, I've chosen Tuscany.
The earth in Sienna isn't as red!

And you?

Spanish misery is so mysterious…

And you?

The trout. The trout. The silence. The water's hair.
A slow and faithful acquaintance as with a woman…

Ah! When will the people of my country…
the respectable people, of course...
receive the little seed of disquiet
which will raise the intolerable anguish of injustice.

Henri Deluy

Mens enfants n'ont pas l'âge de raison
Ils vont au pas
Portés par les saisons
L'amour aux lèvres
Comme une aile de pigeon
Le parfum ouvert sur les yeux

Ce matin où j'ai reconnu ton nom
Ils jouaient devant moi
A qui grandirait plus vite
A qui serait le plus fort

Je n'ai rien voulu dire de ta mort
Son horreur
Ses beffrois
La terre au loin
Le ciel à l'étroit

Pour le moment ils apprennent à lire
A dire les choses comme elles sont

Un jour
Ils se souviendront

Henri Deluy

My children haven't come of age
They go at walking pace
Carried by the seasons
Love on their lips
Like the wing of a pigeon
Perfume open on their eyes

This morning when I recognised your name
They were playing in front of me
At who will grow the quickest
Who will be the strongest

I didn't want to mention your death
Its horror
Its belfries
The land in the distance
The sky close by

For the moment they are learning to read
To say what things are really like

One day
They will remember

Jo Guglielmi

Celui qui prend la garde dans nos rêves
Dans le sang trouble de nos rêves
Celui qui erre à toute heure et ses plaies toujours vertes
Ce fantôme étranglé
Celui qui suffoque sous le cuir pour nous pour toujours
Celui qui va dans l'écume et le sel du supplice
Notre douleur Tais-toi à présent Et toi parfum de la colère

Une maison en construction et un maillot de corps oublié qui avait servi de baillon
Quelqu'un est mort
Nous savons bien dans quelle ville quelle rue dans quelle maison
Une cellule reste vide
Nous savons bien qui a tué

Jo Guglielmi

The one who stands guard in our dreams
In the troubled blood of our dreams
The one who wanders at all hours whose wounds are always raw
This strangled ghost
The one who suffocates under leather for us for always
The one who goes into the foam and the salt of punishment
Our pain be quiet for the moment And you perfume of anger

A house under construction and a forgotten top which had been used as a gag
Someone is dead
We know in which town which street in which house
A cell remains empty
We know very well who did the killing

André Liberati

Celui qui donne au bien son âme
Que pourrait-il craindre en ce monde
Le vent peut éteindre la flamme
La cendre se mêler au vent
Il peut mourir dès à présent
Que pourrait-il craindre en ce monde
Il a vécu il a mangé
Le pain rayonnant des journées
Il a vécu en souriant
Que pourrait-il craindre en ce monde
Il peut vieillir et ressembler
A la poussière du sentier
Il peut mourir en combattant
Il peut mourir assassiné
Que pourrait-il craindre en ce monde
Celui dont l'âme fut donnée

André Liberati

He who gives himself to good
What would he have to fear in this world
The wind can put out the flame
The ash mix with the wind
He could die right now
What could he fear in this world
He has lived he has eaten
The radiant bread of days
He has lived smilingly
What could he fear in this world
He can grow old and resemble
The dust of the track
He can die fighting
He can die by assassination
What could he fear in this world
He who gave himself to good

Henri Merlen

Audin, jamais plus les campanules ne sonneront
Les soirs de tes jours studieux
Jamais plus ne voleront les arabesques lucides
Des chiffres et des formes
La mort est un mot lourd
Un mot sombre
Pour ceux qui ne croient qu'en la vie
Mourir dans la fureur des bêtes
Fait une ombre immortelle
Mort? Ce mot lourd
Ce mot sombre n'est pas pour toi
Vois: ils ont les murailles, la flamme, le fer,
Pour les défendre des fantômes étranglés
Mutilés, égorgés.
Vois: ta place devant eux est vide
Et ils ont peur.

Henri Merlen

Audin, never again will the campanulas ring
In the evening of your studious days
Never again will the lucid arabesques fly
From figures and forms
Death is a heavy word
A grim word
For those who believe only in life
To die in bestial fury
Make an immortal shadow
Death? This heavy word
This grim word is not for you
See: they have the defensive walls, flame, iron
To defend them from strangled ghosts
Mutilated, their throats slit.
See: your place in front of them is empty
And they are afraid.

Jean Pérol
L'ordre

I

La minutieuse floraison d'une idée
La journée tamisée au crible du mystère
La longue main calme de la patience
Qui reprend les pages de la passion
Cette élégance de cygne de la conscience
Chaque mot placé sur sa trajectoire
Tout le savoir d'un seul que les autres partagent
Ce silence qui juge cet équilibre qu'ils détestent
Ils le tiennent enfin entre leurs mains de carnage
Et frappent.

II

Le bien ils le frappent ils le brûlent ils lui crachent dessus
Ils le gonflent d'eau ils le cognent aux murs
Ils le jettent, pour de sauvages curées à la meute électrique
Ils boivent longuement sa douleur au goulot
Et la peau qui saigne soulage leur honte.

III

Les muscles tendus pour la force d'un corps
La chair brute pesant dans l'élan de la haine
Le fauve enragé dans la cage de la tête
La giclée incandescente de la cruauté
Ont toujours volatilisé la lumière
Calciné le souffle la tendresse aux mains nues
Le combat est trop inégal l'issue trop certaine
A quand le triomphe éblouissant de l'amour
A quand l'accueil amical la main tendue du respect
Lorsque la pensée sonne à votre porte

Deux mains qui serrent
La lumière au cou
Font toujours la nuit.

Jean Pérol

Order

I

The scrupulous blooming of an idea
The day woven into the sieve of mystery
The long calm hand of patience
Which takes hold of the pages of passion
This swan-like elegance of conscience
Each word placed in its trajectory
All the knowledge of one who is shared by others
This silence which judges this balance they hate
They hold it finally between their bloody hands
And they strike

II

They strike the good they burn it they spit on it
They swell it with water they smash it against walls
They throw it, for savage priests into the electric mob
They drink long from its pain straight from the bottle
And the bleeding skin relieves their shame.

III

Muscles tensed for the force of a body
The brute flesh weighing in the leap of hate
The mad deer in the head's cage
Cruelty's incandescent spurt
Have always made light disappear
Charred breath tenderness with naked hands
The battle is too unequal the outcome too certain
Till when love's stunning triumph
Till when the friendly welcome the hand offered in respect
When thought knocks on your door

Two hands that clasp
Light on the neck
Always bring night.

Jean Perret

Mon poème est un hurlement. Je le sais. Je le veux.
Toi, je te reconnais
C'est pourquoi les mots fleuris les images
    précieuses, moi, je les casse et m'en garde,
    à cause du sang
Toi, je te reconnais
Toi, tu n'as pas attendu déguisé
Toi, tu n'as pas changé les thèses
Toi, tu n'as pas demandé aux Moudjahidines
    s'ils avaient la carte du Parti et l'autorisation
    de se battre dans les rangs de l'Internationale de Lénine.
Toi, tu les as reconnus les moudjahidines
Ali Boumendjel
Fernand Yveton
Ben M'hidi
Djamila
Alleg et les Guerroudj…
Toi, tu as dit à ton ami: « C'et dur, Henri »
    et puis tu as souri. Henri Alleg et toi, vous avez souri.
C'est alors que les mains sanglantes d'un officier français
    ont étranglé ton sourire

Maurice Audin, j'écris ton nom
Je porte ton nom dans ma colère
Sur mon cœur et ma raison
Ma femme porte ton nom
Mes enfants portent ton nom

Lénine porte ton nom

Jean Perret

My poem is a howl. I know. I want it to be.
You, I recognize you
That's why flowery words precious
    images, me, I break them and am wary of them,
    because of the blood
You, I recognize you
You, you didn't wait in disguise
You, you didn't change the theories
You, you didn't ask the Moujahadines
    if they had a Party card and the authorisation
    to fight in the ranks of Lenin's International
You, you recognised the moujahadines
Ali Boumendjel
Fernand Yveton
Ben M'hidi
Djamila
Alleg and the Guerroudji…
You, you said to your friend: 'It's hard, Henri'
    and then you smiled. Henri Alleg and you, you smiled.
That was the moment the bloody hands of a French officer
    strangled your smile

Maurice Audin, I write your name
I carry your name in my anger
On my heart and my reason
My wife carries your name
My children carry your name

Lenin bears your name

Charles Dobzynski

Chaque mort avait son visage et quel visage
    s'est levé dont la bouche brûle épelant le
    nom en feu d'une patrie

De quelle patrie parlez-vous ces visages sont
    étrangers dont vous exhumez le reflet et
    la lumière basanée

Ces visages sont étrangers à qui je dénie
    aujourd'hui le choix même de la patrie

Ali Mohammed et Malek

Je vous laisse au Pont de l'Enfer est-ce le
    nom de la patrie que vous cherchez dans
    la montagne

Est-ce le nom de la patrie qui prend
    naissance sur vos lèvres
Je vous laisse au Pont de l'Enfer parmi les
    morts qui vous ressemblent

Vos visages entrelacés aux frondaisons de
    notre ciel
Ali Mohammed et Malek.

Je vous laisse au Pont de l'Enfer Vos yeux
    seront rapatriés vos visages prendront
    racine éveillant mille autres visages

Vos visages prendront patrie quand nous
    aurons chassé l'enfer

Charles Dobzynski

Each death had its face and which face
   arose whose mouth burns spelling out
   the burning name of the homeland

Which homeland are you speaking of these faces are
   foreigners whose reflection and dark light
   you exhume

These faces are strangers who today I deny
   even the choice of a homeland

Ali Mohammed and Malek

I leave you at Hell's Bridge is it
   the name of the homeland you are looking for
   in the mountain

Is it the name of the homeland which is
   born on your lips
I leave you at Hell's Bridge amongst
   the dead who look like you

Your faces entwined with the foliage of
   our sky
Ali Mohammed and Malek

I leave you at Hell's Bridge Your eyes
   will be sent home your faces will take root
   awakening a thousand other faces

Your faces will find their homeland when we have
   swept away hell

Oliven Sten

Poème pour les chiens Kabyles

Il n'y a qu'un sang qui coule actuellement.
J.C. Paupert

C'est le même sang un peu pétri d'argile
et si la terre en veut c'est qu'elle est habituée
c'est qu'elle aime le lait et le miel de ce sang
le seul miroir de nos combats séchés

C'est le même sang un peu mélangé d'huile
qui ici-bas coule selon le temps
et comme se règlent à la lune les marées
ce sang-là monte et baisse à la Criée.

Maîtres, voici longtemps déjà vous nous avez appris
que la terre tourne et que la chlorophylle
rend notre mort utile aux végétaux
vous nous avez montré des musées plus fertiles
où les enfants d'Hercule un jour pourront jouer
après les sept travaux.
J'ai compté jusqu'à cent et d'autres jusqu'à mille

Ici rien n'a changé
Il y a dans le duvet des nuits sous toute pierre
Un lézard de détresse
Qui siffle avec nos voix
Des morts qui nous repoussent
De leurs doigts barbelés.

Ici rien n'a changé sinon les chiens kabyles
Qui aboyaient mais ne mordaient pas
Ils mordent sans aboyer
Leurs maîtres sont à la guerre
Eux se roulent sous nos convois.

Oliven Sten

Poem for the Dogs of Kabylie

There is only one blood flowing today.
J.C. Paupert

It's the same blood somewhat kneaded with clay
and if the earth resents it it's because it's used to it
it's because she loves the milk and honey of this blood
the only mirror of our dried out battles

It's the same blood somewhat mixed with oil
which here runs according to the weather
and as the moon rules the tides
this blood rises and falls as I auctioned.

Teachers, for a long time you've been teaching us
that the earth revolves and that chlorophyll
makes our death useful for vegetables
you showed us more productive museums
where Hercules's children one day will be able to play
after the seven challenges.
I have counted to a hundred and others to a thousand

Here nothing has changed
There is in the quilt of night under all stone
A crack of distress
Which whistles with our voices
Deaths which repulse us
With their barbed fingers.

Here nothing has changed except for the dogs of Kabylie
Which barked but never bit
They bite without barking
Their masters are fighting war
Them they roll beneath our convoys.

Maîtres la poésie n'est pas faite pour les chiens
Vous nous avez appris en classe le matin
Que la haine n'est plus que le bras mort des fleuves
Et sur ce tableau noir la craie donne l'onglée
Et je n'endure pas cette guerre sans fin
Et je me sens honteux comme un mauvais élève.

Teachers poetry isn't written for dogs
You taught us in class this morning
That hatred is nothing more than the dead arm of rivers
And on this blackboard the chalk scratches like a fingernail
And I can't endure this endless war
And I feel ashamed like a bad pupil.

Jo Guglielmi
Algérie interdite

Pourtant je t'ai tout confié
La ville comme une lampe sur l'eau
Ses souliers de fatigue
Les voix qui battent l'estrade
Tout le désespoir et son contraire
Derrière la mer cette fille interdite
Ce pays interdit de séjour dans son ciel

Comme j'ai tout confié à la nuit
Les mots qui charrient des fantômes
Le café le tabac le temps pour aimer
Cette enfant les yeux ouverts qui pleure

Jo Guglielmi

Forbidden Algeria

All the same I disclosed everything
The town like a lamp on the water
Its walking shoes
The voices which hammer the stage
All the despair and its opposite
Behind the sea this forbidden girl
This forbidden holiday country in its sky

As I confided everything to the night
The words which carry ghosts
The café the tobacco the time to love
This child crying with its eyes open

Jean-Jacques Viton

Les faits

Le paysage authentique de la paix
Est remis à plus tard.

Le souvenir demeure
Qu'il éclate…

Vivre dans des puits d'horreur
Prendre le jour sur des margelles de crainte
Soude à tous les hommes
Un regard qui n'est pas le nôtre.

*

On en arrive à se demander
Si les mots si les outils du langage
Gardent leur signification.
J'en arrive à ne plus prononcer
Certains mots – Joie ou bien Amour –
A ne plus arriver à les prononcer
Car je porte au plus chaud de ma gorge
Un cri insoutenable intransportable
Qui empoisonne mon sang.

Voici les faits amassés dans ce cri:

Attachée par la cheville
A un piquet de bête
Désespérée hurlante
Vomissant son cri dans l'Histoire
Attachée par ceux qui l'aiment
Et qui ne veulent pas perdre son corps,
Horrible rendue hors les hommes,
Transportant l'horreur sur ses mains déformées
Rendue folle à lier
Par la Guerre

Jean-Jacques Viton

The Facts

The authentic landscape of peace
Is postponed.

Memory remains
Till it shows itself...

Living in pits of horror
Accepting the day on curb-stones of fear
Solder of all men
A look which is not ours.

*

We get to the point of asking
If words if the tools of language
Keep their meaning.
I get to the point of no longer pronouncing
Certain words – Joy or even Love –
No longer being able to pronounce them
Because in the depths of my throat
I bear an unbearable immovable cry
Which poisons my blood.

Here are the facts gathered in this cry:

Fastened by the heel
To an animal's stake
Despairing howling
Vomiting his cry into History
Fastened by those who love him
And who don't want to lose his body,
Horrible arrival outside humanity,
Carrying horror in his deformed hands
Made fit to be tied
By the War

Que mon pays fait au sien
Devenue cette bête entravée
Dans l'ombre fulgurante anéantissante
Des avions
Que mon pays détache contre le sien

Une jeune fille – ce qui fut une jeune fille –
Peut-être l'âge de ma sœur
Rendue hors les hommes
Rendue hors le monde.

Puis-je nommer d'autres voix
Laisser passer avant ce cri
La voix de ceux que j'aime
Quand je porte sur la joue
Cette évidente cocarde de sang?

*

Le paysage de la paix
Tel que nous l'entendons
Est remis à demain.

Je vivrai comme un homme
Dans ce paysage authentique
Lorsque la peur la souffrance
Les armes automatiques
La haine la torture
Les cris les cris
Les viols la faim la faim
L'humiliation la folie le suicide
Seront devenus
Une impalpable cendre froide
Inapte à garder une empreinte.

Nous saurons alors la vie pour laquelle nous sommes faits

Et ce que l'homme est à l'homme.

Octobre 1960

My country built on his
Turned into this shackled beast
In the flashing shadow annihilating
Planes
My country unleashes against his

A young girl – what was a young girl –
Perhaps the age of my sister
Arrived outside humanity
Sent out of the world.

Can I name other voices
Let go by before this cry
The voice of those I love
When I carry on my cheek
This conspicuous rosette of blood ?

*

The landscape of peace
As we understand it
Has been postponed…

I will live like a man
In this authentic landscape
When fear and suffering
Automatic weapons
Hatred torture
Cries and cries
Rapes hunger hunger
Humiliation madness suicide
Have become
An untouchable cold cinder
Unable to retain an impression.

We will know then the life we were made for

And what man is to man.

October 1960

Alain Lance

pour F.T.

Toute la nuit
le vent a cogné aux vitres
et déchiré les affiches de la guerre

mais ce matin
les gens dorment
derrière leurs carreaux rouges
dans leur tasse de tilleul

arbres dépouillés immobiles
tandis que la boue élève ses barricades

la ville au loin
glacée
sans défense

et ton visage perdu dans le camion
c'est déjà la guerre

2 Novembre 1960

Alain Lance

for F.T.

All night
the wind has been bashing the windows
and ripping the war posters

but this morning
the people are sleeping
behind their red tiles
in their cups of herbal tea

stripped motionless trees
while the mud builds its barricades

the town in the distance
frozen
defenceless

and your face lost in the lorry
the war is already here

2 November 1960

Jean Pérol

Dit sans poésie de la colère

Madame

La nuit secoue ses flammes
la peau du visage cuit
c'est l'incendie qui suce les poutres
à droite à gauche des nébuleuses de cris
une ombre court un claquement la poursuit
la couleuvre de sang glisse entre les pierres
un peu partout
car, madame,
votre fils a la gorge tranchée.

Jean Pérol

Said Without Poetic Anger

Madam

The night shakes its flames
the baked face's skin
it's fire which suck the beams
to right and left clouds of screams
a short shadow a clicking in pursuit
the snake of blood slides between the stones
just about everywhere
because, madam,
your son's throat has been cut.

Antoine Vitez

Lettre après plus de quatre ans

Loin de toi,
bien-aimée, douce
comme on dit « la douce France »
je n'ai pas reconnu sur l'asphalte mon ombre longue.
Sur le revêtement français de la route africaine,
Mon ombre n'est plus ni à moi ni à toi, menaçante,
Meurtrière.
Je n'ai pas vu mon visage,
Ni mes mains.
Ne comptent ni mon visage
(mon visage,
bien-aimée),
ni mes mains,
qui te faisaient peur,
te faisaient mal.
Mon ombre, miroir ennemi,
Détestable, où se noient les beaux sentiments,
Bardée dont le fusil dépasse,
Fait la guerre.

Paris, 1960

Antoine Vitez

Letter after More than Four Years

Far from you,
dearly-loved, sweet
as they say 'sweet France'
I didn't recognise my long shadow on the tarmac.
On the French covering of the African road.
My shadow is no longer threatening to me or you,
No longer murderous.
I didn't see my face,
Nor my hands
My face doesn't count any more
(my well-loved
face)
nor my hands,
which frightened you.
My shadow, enemy mirror,
Detestable, where beautiful sentiments
drown,
Armour the rifle pokes out from
Making war.

Paris, 1960

Yves Broussard

Algérie 60

D'un bout à l'autre de la nuit des « camarades » se levaient pour aller tuer dans leur lit les hommes qu'on ne leur demandait pas de tuer le jour...

L'un d'eux exhibait un crâne qu'il ramassa lui-même sous le sable où d'autres l'avaient laissé. Avec son couteau il arrachait les derniers lambeaux de chair dont les crabes ne voulurent pas...

Tout dernièrement un ami de collège rencontré par hasard m'avoua que ce qui lui manque le plus maintenant qu'il est de nouveau civil est « la possibilité de tuer »

Tous les mots ne sont pas bons à dire
Mais ce que je dis de la mort je le dirai un jour de la vie
Rien n'a d'importance désormais que la fin de cette guerre
Paix
Paix sur les murs et les visages
– Ma mémoire s'agite –
Paix dans le creux de chaque main d'homme

Car ni le vent ni la pluie ni l'écoulement des jours
Ne trouveront jamais d'autre explication à mon insomnie
Et ni la joie ni le bonheur ne me feront oublier ce ciel
A peine plus grand qu'un buvard tout tâché d'encre et de sang
Qu'aujourd'hui plus que d'habitude m'est lourd à supporter

O mes amis des quatre horizons

A qui je n'ai pas encore tout dit.

Yves Broussard

Algeria 60

From one end of the night to the other 'comrades' got up to go and kill in their beds men they hadn't been asked to kill during the day..

One showed off a skull he picked up himself under the sand where others had left it. With his knife he cut away the last shreds of flesh the crabs didn't want…

Just lately a school friend I met by chance admitted that what he misses most now he's a civilian is 'the chance to kill'

Not all words are good to speak
But what I say of death one day I will say of life
Nothing matters henceforth but the end of this war
Peace
Peace on walls and faces
– My memory stirs –
Peace in the hollow of every man's hand

Because neither the rain nor the passing of the days
Will ever find a different explanation for my insomnia
And neither joy nor happiness will make me forget this sky
Hardly any bigger than a blotting paper stained with blood and ink
And today more than ever difficult to tolerate

Oh my friends from the four corners of the earth

Who I haven't yet told everything.

G.-L. Godeau

L'encre rouge

Torse nu, un conscrit s'avance sur l'estrade.

L'officier le toise. « Et toi, quels sont tes signes particuliers ? »

Le visage du garçon s'illumine. « Je suis pacifiste. »
L'officier ramasse la bombe. « Pacifiste, demain tu seras soldat. Au suivant. »

Ce soir, au café Bonaparte, le baby-foot est silencieux.
Les enfants à barbe sont assis en rond et parlent à voix basse de choses militaires.
Ils ont des mines graves.

Le suivant a vu l'officier qui encadrait un nom, à l'encre rouge.

G.-L. Godeau

Red Ink

Naked from the waist a conscript goes up on stage.

The officer looks him up and down. 'And you, what are your special qualities?'

The boy's face lights up. 'I'm a pacifist.'
The officer picks up the grenade. 'Pacifist tomorrow you'll be a soldier. Next.'

Tonight, in the café Bonaparte, the table football is quiet.
The bearded children are sitting in a circle and talk in hushed voices of military matters.
They have serious expressions.

The next up saw the officer circle a name in red ink.

Henri Meschonnic

Par le fer et le feu

Des cheveux blonds aux branches nues des pierres tremblent.
Vois-les confondus en terre

Les gestes creux
Les ventres de ta vie
Dans ce sol en remous où se fondent des os
Terre crayeuse écorchée de sang ta légende.
Les cris de ces yeux
Sont les gouttes d'herbe de ton amour
Et tu plonges les bras dans le vivier des morts.

*

Tous ces corps déversés dans ce torrent de rocs
Comme une pluie tarie

La peau des cris comme une plaie
Près de leur bouche
Et tes yeux de jeunesse
La mer ensemencée

Et le sang vide, dur, sur ces cheveux collés.

Henri Meschonnic

By Iron and Fire

Blond hair in the naked branches stones tremble.
See them mingled with the earth

Empty gestures
The guts of your life
In this moving ground where bones melt
Chalky ground scorched with blood your inscription.
The cries of these eyes
Are the drops of your love
And you plunge your hands in the fish-pond of the dead.

*

All these bodies discharged into this torrent of rocks
Like withheld rain

The skin of cries like a wound
Near their mouth
And your youthful eyes
The sea sown with seed

And the empty, hard blood on this matted hair.

Henri Meschonnic

Pour voir clair

Montre tes mains de paix.
Et le sable et les cèdres
Et le feu de tes blés.
Tu as perdu le compte des douleurs.
Tu cries comme une mère.
Les morts n'ont pas besoin de draps.
Vois ceux qui te palpent de leur rire.

Le soleil
Colle les mouches sur ta peau.

Les gestes de ta misère
Pressent ta peur contre la peau.

Le visage de la guerre
A pris la forme de tes os.
Sage
Tu ne chasses plus les mouches
Des yeux de tes enfants

Dans les berceaux de pensées mortes.

Henri Meschonnic

To See Clearly

Show your hands of peace.
And the sand and the cedars
And the fire of your corn.
You've lost the tally of your pain.
You scream like a mother.
The dead don't need sheets.
See those who examine you with their laughter.

The sun
Sticks flies to your skin.

The gestures of your misery
Press your fear against your skin.

The face of war
Has taken the shape of your bones.
Well-behaved
You no longer chase flies
From the eyes of your children

In the cradles of dead thoughts.

Algerian Poets and
the War of Liberation

Noureddine Aba

Mon frère,
L'avions-nous rêvé ce soir
Qui se ferait souffle éperdu,
Rire de source, douceur d'aveu,
Malgré le crépitement des balles?
Mon frère,
L'avions-nous rêvé l'aurore
Pourpre de l'agonie des idoles
Traversée de migrations
Hésitantes d'oiseaux verts,
Malgré le crépitement des balles?
Mon frère,
L'avions-nous rêvé ce silence,
Le silence des rocs surpris,
Ce cri pur du haut des Djebels
Dégrafant les espaces,
Et ce crépitement de balles
Qui annulerait notre honte?
Mon frère,
L'avions-nous rêvé cet instant
Où nos regards sans larmes
Fixeraient la même promesse de printemps,
Malgré le crépitement des balles?
L'avions-nous rêvé, mon frère?
Alors ne pleure pas ma mort.
Au nom du Très Miséricordieux,
Va dire à la mechta saccagée
A la poitrine défoncée,
Au fou qui montre ses poings au soleil,
Au taudis labouré par le char,
Au mendiant à l'heure de la faim
Foudroyé par un obus,
A l'enfant captif des chevaux de frise,
Va leur dire que nous avions rêvé
Cet instant aveugle et de glace

Noureddine Aba

My brother
Had we dreamt of this
Madly blowing evening,
Life-spring of laughter, the sweetness of avowal,
In spite of the bullets' crackling?
My brother,
Had we dreamt of the dawn
Purple with the agony of idols
Crossed by the hesitant migrations
Of green birds,
In spite of the bullets' crackling?
My brother,
Had we dreamt of this silence,
The silence of surprised rocks,
This pure cry from the heights of Djebels
Undoing distances,
And this crackling of bullets
Which would wipe out our shame?
My brother,
Had we dreamt of this moment
When our looks without tears
Would fix on the same promise of spring,
In spite of the bullets' crackling?
Had we dreamt it my brother?
So don't cry for my death.
In the name of the Most Merciful
Go and tell the pillaged village?
The crushed chest
The madman showing his fists to the sun,
The shanty crushed by the tank,
The beggar in his famished hour
Struck down by a shell
The child captured by the horses in a freize,
Go and tell them we had dreamt
This blind, frozen moment

Jusqu'où l'angoisse s'est hissée,
Va leur dire au nom du Très Clément
Que j'exige que ma mort
Soit l'heure du simple amour
Et du secret sussur!
Malgré le crépitement des balles!

Until anguish stood upright,
Go and tell them in the name of the Most Forgiving
That I demand my death
Be the time of simple love
And of the whispered secret!
In spite of the bullets' crackling!

Jean El Mouhoub Amrouche

Le combat algérien

Alors vint une grande saison de l'histoire
Portant dans ses flancs une cargaison d'enfants indomptés
Qui parlèrent un nouveau langage
Et le tonnerre d'une fureur sacrée:
On ne nous trahira plus
On ne nous mentira plus
On ne nous fera plus prendre des vessies peintes
De bleu de blanc et de rouge
Pour les lanternes de la liberté
Nous voulons habiter un nom
Vivre ou mourir sur notre terre mère
Nous ne voulons pas d'une patrie marâtre
Et des riches reliefs de ses festins

Nous voulons la patrie de nos pères
La langue de nos pères
La mélodie de nos songes et de nos chants
Sur nos berceaux et sur nos tombes
Nous ne voulons plus errer en exil
Dans le présent sans mémoire et sans avenir

Ici et maintenant
Nous voulons
Libres à jamais sous le soleil dans le vent
La pluie ou la neige
Notre patrie Algérie

Jean El Mouhoub Amrouche

The Algerian Struggle

Then arrived a great historical moment
Carrying in its flanks a cargo of indomitable children
Who spoke a new language
And the thunder of a sacred fury:
We will no longer be betrayed
We will no longer be lied to
We will no longer be made to believe
The moon is made of red, white and blue cheese
And is a beacon of freedom
We want to live in a name
Live or die on our mother earth
We want nothing to do with a cruel stepmother homeland
And the rich outlines of her feasts

We want the homeland of our fathers
The language of our fathers
The melody of our dreams and our songs
Over our cradles and our graves
We no longer want to wander in exile
In the present without memory or future

Here and now
We want
Free for ever beneath the sun in the wind
The rain or the snow
Our homeland Algeria.

Djamal Amrani

Sous un tas de décombres

pour Ali la Pointe

Ici où chaque jour appelait la souffrance
Ici où chaque pas liait nos volontés d'espoir
Ici où tout criait malheur violence famine
Ici où sourdement le sang se vérifiait et la peine se gagnait
Il a péri. Il a péri enseveli sous un tas de décombres
Alors qu'il piétinait les haines de son sang large
Pour que les racines de son peuple impatient
Se fassent à l'orée du Drapeau
O larmes grises lentes à refroidir
O patiences incurvées jusqu'au feu sacré
Parce qu'ils ont voulu condamner aux ténèbres
Nos marches longues et arides
Parce qu'ils ont voulu déchirer nos vies aux frontières de l'oubli
Ali La Pointe, fils d'une patrie en armes
L'unique des pénitences, le trouble des nuits spacieuses
Terrassait l'infâme dévorait le mépris
Aux premiers signes des fusils.

Djamal Amrani

Under a Pile of Rubble

for Ali la Pointe

Here where each day hailed suffering
Here where each step linked our will to hope
Here where everything screamed unhappiness violence famine
Here where sounding dully blood proved itself and pain was achieved
He perished. He perished buried beneath a heap of rubble
While he was treading the hatreds of his broad blood
So that the roots of his impatient people
Might take at the edge of the Flag
O grey tears slow to cool
O patience turned in on itself as far as the sacred fire
Because they wanted to condemn to the shadows
Our long and arid marches
Because they wanted to shred our lives on the borders of forgetfulness
Ali La Pointe, son of a homeland at war
Unique among repentances, the disturbance of spacious nights
Laid low the vile devoured contempt
At the first sign of rifles

Le voici qui accuse au rassemblement du jour
Les souffles nourris de sang; il est là
Pour ceux qui connaissent l'univers à l'heure grave
Des Servitudes
O furies d'un même passé!
Son visage – miroir de cruautés – où en chœur des cris
Soudent l'espérance, aiguise nos libertés
Le voici encore otage vivant dans les rides de nos
Yeux où le soleil nouveau a chassé à jamais la honte
Et le néant. Je dis: fruits creusés, tavelés, raffinés.
On ensemence car la mort se dédie
Car la mort est plus forte que la faim
O Mère patrie il t'a nommée Certitude avant l'extase
Puis il s'est livré aux flammes afin que soit rendu
Ton souverain éclat

Hier encore sanglé par l'insulte des seigneurs
Englouti par l'inceste misère
Il a aimé les humbles affranchi les tendresses
Consumé le passé
A l'heure multiple de l'héritage
Quand nos joies égrènent les libertés présentes
Quand son nom se chuchote dans le silence de nos voix
Je crie: Enfant de la Casbah
Dégel de nos remparts
Tu as brisé la maille des jardins interdits

Here he is at the day's assembly
The winds nourished by blood; he is here
For those who know the universe in a serious time
Slaveries
O furies of the same past!
His face – mirror of cruelties – where in a chorus screams
Join hope, sharpen our freedoms
Here he is once more living hostage in the furrows of our
Eyes where the new sun has chased away for ever shame
And nothingness. I say: hollowed fruits, blemished, refined
We sow because death dedicates itself
Because death is stronger than hunger
O Motherland he called you Certainty before ecstasy
Then he gave himself up to the flames so
Your sovereign lustre could be realised

Yesterday still thrashed by the lords' insult
Engulfed by incest misery
He loved the humble set free tenderness
Consumed the past
At the complex time of inheritance
When our joys seed today's freedoms
When his name is whispered in the silence of our voices
I cry: Child of the Casbah
Defrost our ramparts
You broke the chain of forbidden gardens.

Messaour Boulanouar

J'écris pour que la vie soit respectée par tous

Je donne ma lumière à ceux que l'ombre étouffe
Ceux qui vaincront la honte et la vermine

J'écris pour l'homme en peine l'homme aveugle
L'homme fermé par la tristesse
L'homme fermé à la splendeur du jour

J'écris pour vous ouvrir à la douceur de vivre

J'écris pour tous ceux qui ont pu sauver
De l'ombre et du commun naufrage
Un coin secret pour leur étoile
Un clair hublot dans les nuages

J'écris pour la lumière qui s'impose
Pour le bonheur qui se révèle
J'écris pour m'accomplir au cœur de mes semblables
Pour que fleurisse en nous le désert froid du mal

J'écris pour que la terre m'appartienne
Chaude tendre et joyeuse

J'écris pour apaiser mon sang
Mon sang violent et dur et lourd de siècles tristes

J'écris pour partager ma joie
Avec ceux qui m'écoutent

J'écris pour être heureux pour être libre
Pour tous les hommes vrais
Qui comprennent mes cris ma peine et mon espoir

Messaour Boulanouar

I write so that life can be respected by all

I give my light to those suffocated by shadow
Those who will triumph over shame and vermin

I write for the man in pain the blind man
The man closed in by sadness
The man hidden from the day's splendour

I write to reveal the sweetness of life to you

I write for all those who have been able to save
From shadow and from the collective shipwreck
A secret corner for their star
A port-hole in the clouds

I write for the light which is indispensable
For the happiness which shows itself
I write to realise myself in the heart of my fellows
So the cold desert of evil within us might come to flower

I write so the earth might belong to me
Warm tender and joyful

I write to quieten my blood
My violent hard and heavy blood of sad centuries

I write to share my joy
With those who listen to me

I write to be happy to be free
For all true men
Who understand my cries my pain and my hope

J'écris pour éveiller l'azur
Au fond des yeux malades
Au fond des vieux étangs de honte

J'écris pour qu'on défende
Pour qu'on respecte
L'arbre qui monte
Le blé qui pousse
L'herbe au désert
L'espoir des hommes

I write to awaken the azur
In the depths of sick eyes
In the depths of old ponds of hatred

I write so we might defend
So we might respect
The tree which rises
The corn which grows
The grass in the desert
The hope of men

Annie Steiner

Ce matin, ils ont osé

Ce matin, ils ont osé
Ils ont osé
Vous assassiner
C'était un matin clair
Aussi doux que les autres
Où vous aviez envie de vivre et de chanter.
Vivre était votre droit
Vous l'avez refusé
Pour que par votre sang d'autres soient libérés.

Nous sommes tristes et meurtries
A travers murs et barreaux
Qui veulent nous séparer
C'est à vous que nous demandons
La force de supporter
L'instant de cruauté
Où tombe le couperet
Puis le coq a chanté

Que vive votre idéal
Et vos sangs entremêlés
Pour que demain ils n'osent plus
Nous assassiner.

Ecrit juste après l'exécution à la guillotine, dans la prison de Barberousse, le 11 février à l'aube 1957, de Mohamed Lakhnache, Mohamed Ouennouni alias « Petit Maroc » et Fernand Yveton.

Annie Steiner

This Morning They Dared

This morning they dared
They dared
Assassinate you
It was a bright morning
As mild as the others
And you wanted to live and sing.
It was your right to live
You refused it
So through your blood others could be free

We are sad and bruised
Through walls and bars
Which want to separate us
It's from you we ask
The strength to tolerate
The moment of cruelty
When the blade falls
Then the cock sang

Let your ideal live
Intermingled with your blood
So that tomorrow they will no longer dare
Assassinate us

Written just after the execution by guillotine, in Barberousse prison, at dawn on 11 February 1957, of Mohamed Laknache, Mohamed Ouennouni alias 'Little Morocco' and Fernand Yveton.

Mohammed Dib

Sur la terre, errante

Quand la nuit se brise,
Je porte ma tiédeur
Sur les monts acérés
Et me dévêts à la vue du matin
Comme celle qui s'est levée
Pour honorer la première eau;

Etrange est mon pays où tant
De souffles se libèrent
Les oliviers s'agitent
Alentour et moi je chante:

Terre brûlée et noire,
Mère fraternelle,
Ton enfant ne restera pas seule
Avec le temps qui griffe le cœur;
Entends ma voix
Qui file dans les arbres
Et fait mugir les bœufs.

Ce matin d'été est arrivé
Plus bas que le silence,
Je me sens comme enceinte,
Mère fraternelle,
Les femmes dans leurs huttes
Attendent mon cri.

Pourquoi, me dit-on, pourquoi
Vas-tu visiter d'autres seuils
Comme une épouse répudiée?
Pourquoi erres-tu avec ton cri,
Femme, quand les souffles
De l'aube commencent
A circuler sur les collines?

Mohammed Dib

On the earth, wandering

When the night breaks
I carry my warmth
On the sharp peaks
And undress in the sight of morning
Like she who rose up
To honour the first water;

Strange is my country where so many
Winds are set free
The olive trees dance
All round and me I sing;

Burnt and black earth,
Fraternal mother,
Your child will not remain alone
With time which claws the heart;
Hear my voice
Which passes through the trees
And makes the oxen bellow.

This summer morning arrived
Lower than silence
I feel as if I'm pregnant,
Fraternal mother,
The women in their huts
Await my cry.

Why, they say to me, why
Are you going to call at other thresholds
Like a rejected bride?
Why do you wander with your cry,
Woman, when the winds
Of dawn begin
To circulate in the hills?

Moi qui parle, Algérie,
Peut-être ne suis-je
Que la plus banale de tes femmes
Mais ma voix ne s'arrêtera pas
De héler plaines et montagnes;

Je descends de l'Aurès
Ouvrez vos portes
Epouses fraternelles,
Donnez-moi de l'eau fraiche,
Du miel et du pain d'orge;

Je suis venue vous voir,
Vous apporter le bonheur,
A vous et à vos enfants;
Que vos petits nouveaux nés
Grandissent,
Que votre blé pousse,
Que votre pain lève aussi
Et que rien ne vous fasse défaut,
Le bonheur soit avec vous.

I who am speaking, Algeria,
Perhaps I'm merely
The most commonplace of women
But my voice won't stop
To hail the plains and the mountains;

I come down from Atlas
Open your doors
Fraternal wives,
Give me fresh water,
Honey and barley bread;

I came to see you
To bring you happiness
You and your children:
Let your little new-born
Grow
Let your corn thrive,
Let your bread rise too
And let nothing be awry,
Happiness be with you.

Anna Gréki

Captif

Captif d'un fou désir de lumière
Je devine avec mes souvenirs
Ce qui demeurera désirable
Quand jaillira le sang des érables
Je vois l'arbre et les portes s'ouvrir
A grand bruit balayant les misères

En guenilles couvertes de terre
Et de sueur dans un cri natal
Qui fait crever les murs partisans
Qui fait claquer l'écorce animale
Des forêts tendues comme un tison
Allant mettre le feu à la mer

Captif dans des cachots plus petits
Que mon corps me voilà affamée
De ce qui m'assouvissait Ma vie
Maintenant réduite à zéro
M'est restée fidèle comme ces chiens
Réduits à ne pas mourir de faim

Captif dans des cachots plus honteux
Que leurs secrets titubant de veille
Et d'impuissance j'entends l'écho
De mes souffrances coupé en deux
Un ami m'est plus cher qu'un héros
Qui mettrait des menottes au soleil

Un jour je vais sortir de la fable
Qui nous empêchait de vieillir
Déployant blessures et sourires
Cœur et colère dans le jour cru
Cette sincérité misérable
Me poigne comme un chien battu

Anna Gréki

Captive

Captive of a mad desire for light
I guess with my memories
What will remain desirable
When the blood of maples will spring forth
I see the tree and the doors opening
With a great noise sweeping away miseries

In rags covered in earth
And sweat in a birthing cry
Which makes partisan walls collapse
Which cracks the animal bark
Of forests tense as a fireband
On its way to set fire to the sea

Captive in dungeons smaller
Than my body here I am starved
Of what satisfied me My life
Now reduced to zero
Has stayed faithful to me like those dogs
Reduced to not dying of hunger

Captive in dungeons more shameful
Than their secrets staggering from sleeplessness
And powerlessness I hear the echo
Of my sufferings cut in two
A friend is dearer to me than a hero
Who will put handcuffs on the sun

One day I am going to leave the fable
Which prevented us from growing old
Deploying wounds and smiles
Heart and anger in the raw day
This miserable sincerity
Stabs me like a beaten dog

Il s'en faudrait de peu que le cœur
Ne me manque certains jours amers
Où je ne sais plus rien retrouver
Des captifs avec moi enchaînés
Ma faim ses raisons et la chaleur
Même de ce désir de lumière

Certains jours amers où je craindrais
Qu'ouvrir les yeux ne me rende aveugle
Alors j'attends que le mal se passe
Car qui dira si je n'ai pas face
A mes regards mon image seule
Captive contre moi déchaînée

It wouldn't take much for me
Not to lose heart on certain bitter days
When I can no longer find anything
Of the captives chained with me
My hunger its reasons and the warmth
Even of this desire for light

Certain bitter days when I would fear
That opening my eyes would make me blind
So I wait for the pain to pass
For who will say if I don't face
My looks my solitary image
Captive unchained against me.

Jean Sénac

Matinale de mon peuple

pour Baya

Tu disais des choses faciles
Travailleuse du matin
La forêt poussait dans ta voix
Des arbres si profonds que le cœur s'y déchire
Et connaît le poids du chant

La tiédeur d'une clairière
Pour l'homme droit qui revendique
Un mot de paix
Un mot à notre dimension

Tu tirais de sa solitude
Le rodeur qui te suit tout pétri de son ombre
Celui qui voudrait écrire comme tu vois
Comme tu tisses comme tu chantes
Apporter aux autres le blé
Le lait de chèvre la semoule,
Et si dru dans le cœur et si fort dans le sang
La bonté de chacun
Le charme impétueux des hommes solidaires

Parle o tranquille fleur tisseuse des promesses
Prélude au sûr éveil de l'orge
Dis que bientôt l'acier refusera la gorge
Bientôt le douar entamera la nuit.

Tu m'apprends à penser
A vivre comme tu es
Matinale arrachée à l'obscure demeure.

Jean Sénac

Morning for my people

for Baya

You said simple things
Woman worker of the morning
The forest grew in your voice
Trees so deep the heart was torn by them
And knew the weight of song

The warmth of a clearing
For the just man who demands
A word of peace
A word of our size

You will draw from his solitude
The prowler who follows you withered in his shadow
He who would like to write how you see
How you weave how you sing
To bring to others corn
Goat's milk semolina,
And so thick in the heart and so strong in the blood
The goodness of each
The impetuous charm of men in solidarity

Speak O peaceful flower weaver of promises
Prelude to the certain appearance of barley
Say that soon steel will refuse the throat
Soon the small village will broach the night.

You teach me to think
To live like you are
Morning torn from your obscure home.

Kateb Yacine

Poussières de juillet

Le sang
Reprend racine
Oui
Nous avions tout oublié
Mais notre terre
En enfance tombée
Sa vieille ardeur se rallume

Et même fusillés
Les hommes s'arrachent de la terre
Et même fusillés
Ils tirent la terre à eux
Comme une couverture
Et bientôt les vivants n'auront plus où dormir

Et sous la couverture
Aux grands trous étoilés
Il y a tant de morts
Tenant les arbres par la racine
Le cœur entre les dents

Il y a tant de morts
Crachant la terre par la poitrine
Pour si peu de poussière
Qui nous monte à la gorge
Avec ce vent de feu

Ainsi qu'un boulet rouge
Aveugle
Sans retour
Quel ancêtre abattu t'oublia dans son crâne
Fleur de poussière éclose aux lèvres du Rhummel
Laitance d'enfant sevré
Qui fit pousser nos dents toutes neuves?

Kateb Yacine

Dust of July

Blood
Takes root again
Yes
We had forgotten everything
But our land
Fallen in infancy
Rekindles her old ardour

And even shot
Men pull themselves from the earth
And even shot
They pull the earth over themselves
Like a blanket
And soon the living will have nowhere to sleep

And under the blanket
In the great starry blanks
There are so many dead
Holding trees by their roots
The heart between teeth

There are so many dead
Spitting earth from their chests
For so little dust
Which rises into our throats
With the wind of fire

Like a red canon ball
Blind
Not coming back
What fallen ancestor forgot you within their skull
Flower of fresh-blown dust with lips of the Rhumel
Milt of the weaned child
Who made our new teeth grow?

Tant de fois abattu
L'ancêtre au loin s'obstine
Sa tête
Au fond du fleuve
Et du soleil
Détale

Et la tête tranchée n'a pas subi d'éclipse
N'a pas cessé de luire ainsi qu'un boulet rouge
Issu d'un autre orage et d'une autre tribu
N'enterrez pas l'ancêtre

Tant de fois abattu
Laissez-le renouer la trame de son massacre
Il ne renonce pas
A déserter son ombre
L'orphelin de Grenade
Mûri en étranger
Ni à faire éclater son cœur entre nos dents
N'enterrez pas l'ancêtre tant de fois abattu
Le cavalier qui gronde et sourit dans son gouffre
Après nous il galope
Rouge et noir jour et nuit
En un renversement amer et lumineux

N'enterrez pas l'ancêtre
Sauvagement abattu
Il ne renonce pas à la lumière
Ce possesseur des renversements amers de l'iris
Tout près du vieux requin
Qu'habitent ses victimes
Près de l'ancêtre muré vif
Gît le secret de l'être
Atroce inespéré

Laid low so many times
The distant ancestor persists
His head
At the bottom of the river
And the heart of the sun
Runs away

And the severed head hasn't suffered eclipse
Hasn't ceased to shine just as a red canon ball
Come from a different storm a different tribe
Don't bury the ancestor

Laid low so many times
Let him refasten the weft of his massacre
He doesn't give up on
Leaving his shadow
The orphan from Grenada
Grown up abroad
Nor on making his heart explode against our teeth
Don't bury the ancestor laid low so many times
The horseman who grumbles and smiles in his pit
He gallops after us
Red and black day and night
In a bitter and shining reversal

Don't bury the ancestor
Savagely laid low
He doesn't give up on the light
This possessor of the bitter reversals of the iris
Very close to the old shark
Its victims inhabit
Near the ancestor buried alive
Lies the secret of being
Atrocious unhoped for

N'enterrez pas l'ancêtre
Il dort
Sur un tableau de roc
Et il déroule d'autres désastres
Pour les adolescents
Assis sous son coursier
Et il retourne l'un après l'autre
Trop de visages d'enfants précoces
Qui auraient pu être les siens
Il suspend dans l'orage
Le rire de la cascade
Sur le Rhummel trahi
Et muet il écoute
Ainsi qu'un ouragan allongé sur sa lance

Mais qu'avons-nous l'un après l'autre à tomber devant lui?

Pareille au javelot tremblant
Qui le transperce
Nous ramenons à notre gorge
La longue escorte des assassins

Don't bury the ancestor
He's sleeping
On a bed of rock
And he unfolds other disasters
For adolescents
Seated on his war-horse
And he returns one after another
Too many faces of precocious children
Who could have been his own
He hangs in the storm
The laughter of the waterfall
On the betrayed and silent Rhummel
He listens
Like a hurricane laid out on his lance

But what are we doing one after another falling before him?

Like a trembling javelin
Which pierces him
We bring back to our throat
The long convoy of the assassins

Henri Kréa

Lettre à un étranger incompréhensible

I

Les discours indigestes les sourires des puissants
L'exercice trop facile des restes de vertu
La pratique burlesque des bruits de la cité
Qui démange ces bêtes plus bêtes qu'un arbre mort

N'oublions pas les récentes douleurs
Les enfants étranglés sans pourtant disparaître
Cette gent minuscule qui vous cirait les chaussures
Les gagne-petit les modestes aux yeux noirs

Ne croyez pas que la terre est offerte
Comme une femme de force prise
Elle vous mangera peut-être
Car la nature n'est pas impunément soumise
Faites ce que vous voulez
Délabrez toutes les vies
Martyrisez les âmes
Jamais vous
N'aurez touché à l'esprit qui ne dort pas

II

La grande loi de ces remords obligatoires
Vous mangerez au râtelier des forts
Dont la vieillesse est terrible
Croyez les histoires du peuple.

Henri Kréa

Letter to an incomprehensible stranger

I

Indigestible speeches the smiles of the powerful
The too easy exercise of the remains of virtue
The ludicrous practice of the noises of the city
Which itches these beasts more stupid than a dead tree

Let's not forget the recent pains
The children strangled without however disappearing
That tiny type who polished your shoes
The pittance-earners the penniless with dark eyes

Don't believe the earth is offered
Like a woman taken by force
She will perhaps eat you
Because nature is not brought to heel without a cost
Whatever you may do
Ruin all lives
Martyr all souls
Never will you
Have touched the spirit which doesn't sleep

II

The great law of these obligatory regrets
You will have a foot in both camps of the powerful
Whose age is terrible
Believe in the histories of the people.

Nourredine Tidafi

La patrie totale

De mon Algérie
ils établirent des prisons plus hautes
que les écoles.
Ils ont souillé les racines nocturnes
du Peuple,
l'Arbre grave
de la Berbérie reculée.

L'injustice s'est faite cordes noueuses
au goût de pluie.

Sur les cahiers de leurs fautes larges,
nocturnes, mon Peuple se lève.
Ecoutez-le. Il accuse avant les haines.
Face à la mer:
« Frères ici même Apatrides
paysans rugueux des Rocailles et de la Soif
Ils ont nié la certitude de notre Terre
ils ont déchiré l'Islam, sa couleur,
ses tribus fantasques, jusqu'à la honte qui les fait vivre

Ils ont nié le Feu Vital, notre Drapeau
Ils ont exilé les joies humbles de nos chaumières
lentes au retour du maïs. »

Sur mon Peuple obstiné
ils ont codifié l'homme en mépris
saccagé nos rêves de pierres rouges
dans nos sommeils.

Sur mon Peuple aux haltes claires
ils ont enterré la Fibre du Sud
dans les puits rauques.

Nourredine Tidafi

The complete homeland

From my Algeria
they establish prisons taller
than schools.
They have sullied the nocturnal roots
of the People,
the serious tree
of the distant Berbers.

Injustice has turned itself into knotted ropes
tasting of rain.

On the notebooks of their wide nocturnal
faults, my People rises up.
Listen to it. It accuses before hatred.
Facing the sea:
'Brothers Stateless in this very place
rough peasants from Rockeries and Thirst
They have denied the certainty of our Land
they have torn up Islam, its colour,
its fantastic tribes, as far as the shame they live by

They have denied the Vital Fire, our Flag
They have exiled the slow humble joys of our cottages
at corn harvest.'

On my obstinate People
they have codified the man of disdain
pillaged our dreams of red rocks
in our sleep

On my People of plain resting-places
they have buried the Southern Fibre
in rough pits.

Le patriarche déshérité de sa sagesse
s'entoure d'hiver et de muraille.

Anonyme, réduit à espérer, mon Peuple
traverse le soleil
sans témoins,
attendu là-bas par le Malheur.
Et la Patrie me reste comme un silence étranger.

Peuple, en toi où tout commence
ils ont écrit leur présence de larmes
de tous les âges: humiliation générale,
incrustée comme un sel
qui reste à chasser de nos veines.

Et dans mon pays l'enfant s'étonne de mourir.

Aveugles! Aveugles!
Sur mon Peuple Illimité
ils choisirent la cravache sans comprendre
le pouvoir des livres,
le rythme de notre sang,
nos droits au sacrifice,
à l'impatience.

Tout notre corps s'y refusait.

Prisonniers de leurs forfaits
ils écoutent le bruit sombre des crosses
qui se mêle au vent
après la poudre.
Sans regards et sans mots
ils désignent la patrouille précise
au milieu des raisins,
sa halte sous l'orgueil noir des pins
au détour des traverses furieuses,
du cri résumé des Patriotes
d'où fond la liberté comme un aigle.

The patriarch disinherited of his wisdom
surrounds himself with winter and high walls.

Anonymous, reduced to hope, my People
crosses the sun
without witnesses,
awaited there by Misfortune.
And the Homeland remains for me like a foreign silence.

People, in you where everything begins
they have written their tearful presence
of all the ages: general humiliation,
incrusted like salt
which remains to be driven from our veins.

And in my country the child is astonished to die.

Blind! Blind!
On my limitless People
they have chosen the riding-whip without understanding
the power of books,
the rhythm of our blood,
our right to sacrifice,
to impatience.

The whole of our body revolted.

Prisoners of their contracts
they listen to the sad sound of their rifle butts
which mingle with the wind
after the gunpowder.
Without looks and without words
they detail the patrol right
in the middle of the grapes,
rest under the pride of our pines
turning away from furious crossings,
from the gathered cry of the Patriots
where freedom is grounded like an eagle.

Toutes chairs réclament leur violence.

Sur le chemin né de la colère et de l'amande douce
Mon Peuple en haillons, debout dans ses droits
organise son Refus,
chuchotant le Futur, de gorge en gorge
parmi les vieux couteaux,
le feu qui se partage…

Au seuil des douleurs et des fruits
mon Peuple affûte sa Révolution.

L'Arbre retourne en terre.

Sur chaque fusil se dit la Patrie
éclairant de son sang nos nuits ennemies.
Là-haut des terres anciennes me traverse
son bruissement dans une odeur sauvage
de prairie au printemps.

Destin sûr d'exister au plus haut!

Fils solitaires des Chotts, Chaouïas précis,
Peuple haut, de premier sang,
riche de martyrs, l'Arbre-Peuple,
Soleil du Territoire m'appelant
au jour multiple, à l'heure des criques,
    du Drapeau et des murmures.
« La Liberté avec tous ses orages
vaut mieux que le calme plat
de la servitude. »

All flesh demands its violence.

On the road born of anger and sweet almond
My People in rags, upright in their rights
organise their Refusal,
whispering the Future, from throat to throat
amongst old knives,
the fire which can be shared…

On the threshold of pain and of fruit
my People sharpens its Revolution.

The Tree returns to the earth.

On every rifle the Homeland is declared
lighting with its blood our enemy nights.
Up there ancient lands go through me
its murmuring in a savage odour
of the meadow in spring.

Destiny sure to exist at the highest level!

Solitary sons of the Schotts, exact Chaouias
Fine People, of the best blood
rich in martyrs, the Arab-People,
Sun of the Territory calling to me
in the various day, at the time of circuses,
   of the Flag and murmurs.
'Freedom with all its storms
is worth more than the flat calm
of servitude.'

Jean Pélegri

Les paroles de la rose

Je ne suis pas responsible de ce poème. Je l'ai composé, en effet, avec des phrases sorties de la bouche d'une vieille femme de ménage algérienne... C'est elle qui m'avait poussé à l'écrire. Elle était le peuple – le vieux peuple algérien avec ses douleurs et son sourire. Elle était la poésie. Et je ne lui ai servi, ici, que de kateb, c'est-à-dire d'écrivain public. Assis à l'ombre d'un mur, devant ses plumes et son écritoire, il rédige sous la dictée de ceux qui ne savent pas écrire. Ensuite, comme le destin, il sèche l'encre – avec un peu de sable. Elle serait heureuse, je crois, si elle savait que sa letter est bien arrivée. Elle s'appelait Fatima.

Le soleil c'est pour le Bon Dieu
Et le feu c'est pour les soldats

Nous sommes tous fous, m'sieur Jean
Dieu nous a tout donné

La main pour caresser
Et elle sert à tuer

La grenade pour la bouche
Et elle sert à mutiler

La terre pour tapis
Et elle sert à enterrer

Pourquoi tout ça, m'sieur Jean
Dieu nous a tout donné

L'arbre pour son ombre
Et elle sert aux embudcades

Le couteau pour le fruit
Et elle sert pour la gorge

Jean Pélegri

The words of the rose

I am not responsible for this poem. I composed it, as a matter of fact, from sentences from the mouth of an old woman from an Algerian household.... It's she who impelled me to write it. She was the people – the old Algerian people with its pains and its smile. She was poetry. And I served her in this merely as a kateb, that is a public writer. Sitting in the shadow of a wall, in front of his pens and his writing-desk, he edits from what those who can't write tell him. Then, like destiny, he dries the ink – with a little sand. She would be happy, I think, if she knew her letter had arrived. She was called Fatima.

The sun is for the Good Lord
And fire is for soldiers

We are all mad, Mister John
God has given all of us

Hands for caressing
And they are used for killing

Shells we can eat from
And we use them to mutilate

The earth for a carpet
And we use it as a burial ground

Why all that, Mister John
God has given all of us

The tree for shade
And we use it for ambushes

The knife for fruit
And we slit throats with it

La nuit pour reposer
Et elle sert à veiller

Nous sommes tous fous, m'sieur Jean
Si tu veux boire la mer
C'est la mer qui te noie

Quand Die te dome un fils
Ce n'est pas pour l'enterrer
Mais tu dois sourire, m'sieur
Le sourire c'est pour les vieilles
Le sourire protégé les vieilles
C'est leur voile de mariée

Nous avions une odeur de jasmin
Et maintenant regarde, m'sieur Jean
Regarde mes bras et mes mains

La main qui sert à caresser
Sert aujourd'hui à mendier

Nous étions rose, jasmine et lilas
Regarde ma bouche et mes cheveux

Le sourire protégé les vieilles
C'est leur voile de mariée

Il ne me rester que mes yeux
Et c'est pour voir mon file tué

Regarde la lune dans le ciel
C'est une branche de palmier

Regarde là-haut cette montagne
Regarde cet avion qui passé
Mons fils aussi l'a regardé

Le soleil c'est pour le bon Dieu
Et le feu pour les soldats

The night for rest
And we use it for vigils

We are all mad, Mister John
If you want to drink the sea
The sea will drown you

When God gives you a son
It's not so you can bury him
But you must smile, Mister John
The smile is for old people
The smile protects old women
It's their wedding veil

We had an odour of jasmine
And now look, Mister John
Look at my arms and my hands

The hand that is used for caressing
Today is used to beg

We were rose, jasmine and lilacs
Look at my mouth and my hair

The smile protects old women
It's their wedding veil

All I have left are my eyes
And they are to see my murdered son

Look at the moon in the sky
It's a branch of a palm tree

Look up there at this mountain
Look at this plane going by
My son also looked at it

The sun is for the Good Lord
And fire for soldiers

Quand Dieu te donne un fils
Ce n'est pas pour l'enterrer
Mais plus haut il y a un figuier
Et une eau qui ne tarit pas
Plus haut il y a un Jardin
Je vais mourir, m'sieur Jean
Regarde la lune qui se fend
Je vais mourir sans mon enfant

Mais il faut sourire, m'sieur
Le sourire protégé les vieilles

On va m'enrouler dans un voile
Et me coucher seule dans la terre

Il faut sourire, m'sieur Jean
C'est mon voile de mariée
Mais si tu marches dans un jardin
Pense à moi, m'sieur Jean
Pense à ta vieille Fatima
Elle a soigné ton enfant
Le sien elle ne l'avait plus

Quand Dieu te donne un fils
Ce n'est pas pour l'enterrer

Pense à moi et puis souris
Moi je serai dans le Jardin

Mais dis qu'on chose, m'sieur Jean
Dis qu'que chose toi qui sais lire
Dis qu'que chose pour les autres
N'aient pas besoin de ce voile
Pour avoir sur terre un jardin.

Alger, 1957

When God gives you a son
It isn't so you can bury him
But higher up there's a fig tree
And a source of water which doesn't dry up
Higher up there's a garden
I'm going to die, Mister John
Look at the moon which splits
I'm going to die without my child

But we must smile, Mister John
The smile protects old women

They will roll me in a veil
And lay me alone in the earth

We must smile, Mister John
It's my bride's veil
But if you walk in a garden
Think of me, Mister John
Think of your old Fatima
She looked after your child
Her own she no longer had

When God gives you a son
It isn't so you can bury him

Think of me and then smile
Me I'll be in the garden

But say something, Mister John
Say something you who know how to read
Say something so the others
Won't need this veil
In order to have a garden on earth.

Algiers, 1957

Malek Haddad

Le droit de dire au monde

Pensées creusées comme un rocher de vagues
Scrupules mis au point
Morale façonnée comme un morceau de pain
Et chaleur méritée d'une main camarade

Paroles qu'on choisit, mot qu'on prend pour un autre
Amour dont on m'a dit qu'il n'était que d'orgueil
Et rose trop couvée dont on fait des orties
Ô sapins condamnés à mort

Et cent mille chandelles
Dans la nuit boréale
Pas une étoile
Dessus la citadelle de sable

Pourtant
Pensées creusées comme un rocher de vagues
Scrupules mis au point

Et l'étonnant linceul de ceux qui ont raison
Pour dénoncer le froid

Malek Haddad

The right to tell the world

Thoughts hollowed out like a rock by waves
Scruples put in question
Morals moulded like a bit of bread
And the deserved warmth of a friendly hand

Words one chooses, a word you mistake for another
Love I was told was nothing but pride
And rose cultivated too long which become nettles
O fir trees condemned to death

And a hundred thousand candles
In the northern night
Not a star
Above the sand citadel

However
Thoughts hollowed out like a rock by waves
Scruples put in question

And the astonishing shroud of those who are right
To denounce the cold

Malek Haddad

Et la paix revenue
La colombe dira
Qu'on me fiche la paix
Je redeviens oiseau.

Malek Haddad

And peace returned
The dove will say
I don't give a fig for peace
I'm a bird again.

Bachir Hadj Ali

Serment

Je jure sur la raison de ma fille attaché
Hurlant au passage des avions
Je jure sur la patience de ma mère
Dans l'attente de son enfant perdu dans l'exode
Je jure sur l'intelligence et la bonté d'Ali Boumendjel
Et le front large de Maurice Audin
Mes frères mes espoirs brisés en plein élan
Je jure sur les rêves généreux de Ben M'hidi et d'Inal
Je jure sur le silence de mes villages surprise
Ensevelis à l'aube sans larmes sans prières
Je jure sur les horizons élargis de mes rivages
A mesure que la plaie s'approfondit hérissée de lames
Je jure sur la sagesse des moudjahidine maîtres de la nuit
Je jure sur la certitude de jour happée par la nuit
    transfigurée par l'aurore
Je jure sur les vagues déchaînées de mes tourments
Je jure sur la colère qui embellit nos femmes
Je jure sur l'amitié vécue les amours différées
Je jure sur la haine et la foi qui entretiennent la flamme
Que nous n'avons pas la haine contre le peuple français

Alger, 15 décembre 1960

Bachir Hadj Ali

Vow

I swear on the sanity of my tethered daughter
Shouting at passing planes
I swear on the patience of my mother
Waiting for her child lost in the exodus
I swear on the intelligence and the goodness of Ali
    Boumendjel
And the wide forehead of Maurice Audin
My brothers my hopes broken as they sprang
I swear on the generous dreams of Ben M'hidi and Inal
I swear on my surprised villages' silence
Buried at dawn without tears without prayers
I swear on the widened horizons of my river banks
As the wound deepens raised by blades
I swear on the wisdom of the moujahdin masters of the night
I swear on the certainty of the day seized by the night
    transfigured by the dawn
I swear on the unleashed waves of my torments
I swear on the anger which makes our women beautiful
I swear on lived friendship deferred loves
I swear on hatred and the faith which keeps the flame burning
That we have no hatred for the French people.

Algiers, 15 December 1960

Algerian poems
translated from Arabic

Omar El Bernaoui

Fierté

Ma fierté est profonde comme les racines du tronc
Et ma hauteur rivalise avec ton sommet,
Ô palmier
J'ai connu en toi le défi
Tu es un maître
J'ai connu en toi la verticalité
Qui, comme moi, a donné sans compter
Et qui, à part toi, est généreux
Tu es allé au-delà de la générosité
Et en toi s'égalent le seigneur et le haineux
Ô palmier, si tu es patient face à la sécheresse
Comment sera ma patience devant la sécheresse du cœur
Toute sécheresse est facile dans l'univers
Sauf celle qu'affronte l'amoureux de la part de sa bien aimée
Ô palmier, il n'est d'autre beauté que de toi
Ta hauteur nage dans ta lumière
Où est la beauté, patrie éternelle
Où chaque jour qui passe ne trouve que toi.

Omar El Bernaoui

Pride

My pride is deep like the roots of the trunk
And my height competes with yours
Oh palm tree
In you I knew defiance
You are a master
In you I knew verticality
Who, like me, has given without counting the cost
And who, apart from you, is so generous
You have surpassed generosity
And in you the lord and the low find equality
Oh palm tree, if you are patient in the face of drought
What will my patience be like before the drought of the heart
All drought in the universe is easy
Except for that which brings affront to the lover from his beloved
Oh palm tree, there is no beauty but yours
Your height swims in your light
Where is the beauty, eternal homeland
Where each day that passes finds only you.

Mohamed Saleh Baouiya

Le révolutionnaire

Ô mes camarades
Mes camarades de la guerre, de la prison, de la tombe, de la souffrance du monde
Le rire de mes chaînes à mes pieds
Ô mes camarades, regardez
La vengeance me dévore la poitrine
Ô la folie de la révolution rouge
Elle passe sur mon être et sur les grottes de mes collines
Ma mère a juré par mes chaînes, par mes blessures
Qu'elle n'essuiera jamais les larmes de mes yeux
Elle a juré de nettoyer la mitraillette, le canon et la hache
Avec la haine populaire
Pour en faire une frappe vierge qui effacera le sourire du tueur
Dans le champ fertile
Elle a juré qu'elle va téter la victoire
Et ma sœur sur le rivage de la mort
Dans l'excitation du feu
Les Aurès de mes rêves sont lourds
Dans les visions du bourreau
Dans les nuits de la prison
Aurès, vous êtes à moi
Dans tout mon être
Et moi l'ouragan dans la fête du tyran
Ô nostalgie des vengeances qui voyage dans mes entrailles
Mes coups sont un feu qui chante avec mes espérances
Je suis fort
Tempête et explosion,
Je porte l'aube dans mes mains
Et je sens le vent qui aboie dans ma poitrine
Dans mon sang, coule leur sang
Dans mes champs et dans mes halètements

Mohamed Saleh Baouiya

The revolutionary

Oh my comrades
My comrades in arms, in prison, in the grave, in the world's suffering
The laughter of my chains at my feet
Oh my comrades, look
Vengeance devours my chest
Oh the madness of the red revolution
It passes over my being and over the caves of my hills
My mother swore by my chains, by my injuries
That she would never wipe the tears from my eyes
She swore to clean the machine gun, the canon and the axe
With popular hatred
To make a virgin blast which will wipe out the killer's smile
In the fertile field
She swore that she'll feed victory
And my sister on the river bank of death
In the excitement of fire
The Atlas of my dreams is heavy
In the executioner's vision
In the prison nights
Atlas, you belong to me
In the whole of my being
And me the hurricane in the tyrant's celebration
Oh nostalgia for the vengeances which travel through my entrails
My blows are a fire which sings with my hopes
I am strong
Storm and explosion
I carry the dawn in my hands
And I feel the wind which howls in my chest
In my blood flows their blood
In my fields and my panting

Se cachent mes camarades dans les plis de la vallée, dans le nuage et dans la cabane du berger
Ils ont pointé leurs canons sur les prisons et ils sont devenus des étoiles filantes
Qui chantent les sensations de la vie.

My comrades are hiding in the folds of the valley, in the cloud and in the shepherd's hut
They aimed their canons at the prisons and they became shooting stars
Which sing life's sensations.

Popular
Algerian poems

Un poème kabyle

J'ai recueilli
Précieusement la perdrix
Et je l'ai ligotée
J'étais heureux
Je croyais l'avoir apprivoisée.

Dieu lui a offert de jolis traits
Elle est plus belle
Que la plus belle
Tout est perfection chez elle.

Las! un jour elle se révolta
Et se sauva chez ses parents.

Je ne puis me résigner à cette séparation…

A Poem from Kabylie

I caught
The partridge with finesse
And I tied it
I was happy
I thought I'd tamed it

God made her pretty
She's more beautiful
Than the most beautiful
Everything about her is perfect

Sad! One day she rebelled
And ran off to her parents.

I can't get used to this separation…

Bwaqel

Souvent, les soirs de pleine lune, les jeunes filles musulmanes d'Alger ou de Blida se réunissent sur les terrasses pour le jeu de la Bouqâla (jeu de la Gargoulette). Après une invocation religieuse rituelle, chacune place les doigts sous la cruche qui se met à tourner tandis que les jeunes filles récitent ou chantent de courts poèmes empruntés à la tradition orale et transposés au gré de leur fantaisie. L'une des récitantes est ensuite chargée de définir le présage ou le message contenu dans le texte qu'elles viennent de recréer.

Ce jeu de poésie divinatoire s'accompagne fréquemment de pratiques magiques. Dans certaines rues de la casbah, par exemple, on remplit la gargoulette, qui doit être neuve, avec l'eau de sept fontaines différentes. On y jette ensuite sept petits morceaux de bois arrachés à sept portes de la maison.

Cette poésie purement populaire et féminine rejoint les grands courants folkloriques de la Méditerranée. Mostefa Lacheraf et Saâdeddine Bencheneb ont publié des recueils de ces chansons de jeunes filles arabes. Nous donnons ici quelques variantes inédites de « bwaqel » entendues en 1950.

Aujourd'hui, les jeunes filles algériennes vivent dans l'angoisse, la mort et le combat. Leurs chants doivent raconter la peine du peuple, les exploits de leurs frères et de leurs bien-aimés, l'espérance tenace. Mais ces chants ne nous sont pas encore parvenus.

Jean Sénac

Bwaqel

Often, in the evenings when the moon was full, the young Muslim girls from Algiers or Blida got together on the patios for the game of Bouqâla (also known as Gargoulette). After a religious invocation, everyone puts their fingers under the jug which begins to turn while the girls recite or sing short poems taken from the oral tradition and transformed according to their wishes. One of the speakers is then asked to define the prediction or the message contained in the text she has just recreated.

This game of poetic divination is often accompanied by magical practices. In some of the streets of the casbah for example, they fill the water cooler, which has to be new, with water from seven different fountains. They then throw in seven little bits of wood taken from seven front doors.

This purely popular and feminine poetry combines with the great folklore currents of the Mediterranean. Mostefa Lacheraf and Saâddine Bencheneb have published collections of these songs by young Arab girls. Here we publish several previously unseen versions of 'bwaqel' heard in 1950.

Today, young Algerian girls live in anxiety, with death and conflict. Their songs have to tell of the people's pain, their brothers' and lovers' exploits, their tenacious hope. But we haven't yet been able to get hold of these songs.

Jean Sénac

Je suis descendue au fond du jardin,
J'ai coupé une branche de citronnier.
Ma mère aime la politesse, mon père aime la religion
Et moi j'aime un jeune homme aux yeux très colorés.
Figure de lune, je le regarde et je détaille tous ses traits.
Je pose sa tête sur mon genou et je lui dis des vers

***

Brun, mon joli brun, tout ce que tu mets te va bien.
Tu descends au port, tu affoles le navigateur,
Tu entres dans la mosquée, surpris les croyants se taisent,
Toi qui as pris la moitié d'Alger et la moitié de Tunis!

***

Ô brun, ô brun! on me raille à cause de toi.
Tu es une bague d'or et moi ton brillant,
Tu es une gandourah de soie et moi une rayure tissée en toi,
Tu es une ceinture et moi ta boucle.
Pour toi je me battrai avec mes bras
Et celle qui gagnera te prendra.

***

J'habite la vallée
Et mon ami habite la montagne.
Mon père m'a voilée et je ne trouve pas de messager.
Je lui enverrai une bague
Avec un rubis aussi rouge que le cou d'un pigeon,
Et notre rencontre aura lieu dans le couloir du hammam.
J'embrasserai sa joue droite
Et je jeûnerai pendant sept jours.

I went down to the bottom of the garden,
I cut a branch from the lemon tree.
My mother likes politeness, my father likes religion
And me I like a young man with very bright eyes
Moon-faced, I watch him and I notice all his features.
I lay his head on my knee and a recite poetry to him

***

Dark one, my pretty dark one, everything you wear suits you.
You go down to the port, you put the seafarer in a panic,
You go into the mosque, surprised the believers go quiet,
You who have conquered half of Algiers and Tunis!

***

Oh dark one, oh dark one! they tease me because of you.
You are a gold ring and me your stone,
You are a silken tunic and me a stripe woven into you,
You are a belt and I your buckle.
For you I will fight with my fists
And she who wins will have you.

***

I live in the valley
And my boyfriend lives in the moutains.
My father veiled me and I can't find a messenger.
I will send him a ring
With a ruby as red as the neck of a pigeon.
And we will meet in the hallway of the sauna
I will kiss his right cheek
And I will fast for seven days.

***

Il est passé devant notre porte en pelant des oranges amères
Il a fait semblant de tomber pour s'asseoir sur le seuil.
Elle lui a demandé: jeune homme qui es-tu?
Je m'appelle Mohammed,
Fils de la Lune, fils de l'esclave Olga.
Sa beauté avait le signe du bonheur.

***

Mohammed, Mohammed,
Aucune femme n'a eu un garçon comme toi!
Ô beauté de ton corps!
Tu n'as jamais été absent de mes pensées.
Je n'ai pas trouvé l'oiseau digne
De t'apporter mon bonjour.

***

Quand il a plu, la grappe a soupiré.
Le croissant de lune a dit: Dois-je enlever les sortilèges
Les nuages ont dit: Tu commettrais un péché,
Laisse les amoureux s'aimer
Jusqu'à ce que Mektoub passe.

***

Ô ma nuit, Fatma! ô ma nuit, Fatoum!
S'il fallait te rejoindre et traverser la mer,
Je bâtirais un pont,
Et si tu étais au ciel,
Je dresserais une échelle!
Pour toi, je suis allé à Alger,
Pour toi j'irais à Rome.

***

He passed our front door peeling bitter oranges
He pretended to fall so he could sit down on the step.
She asked him: young man who are you?
I'm called Mohammed,
Son of the Moon, son of Olga the slave.
His beauty bore the hallmark of happiness.

***

Mohammed, Mohammed,
No woman has had a boy like you!
Oh the beauty of your body!
You have never been out of my thoughts.
I couldn't find a bird worthy
Of bringing you my greeting.

***

When it rained, the bunch of grapes sighed.
The moon's crescent said: Must I remove the charms?
The clouds said: You will commit a sin,
Let the lovers love one another
Until Mektoub passes.

***

Oh my night, Fatima! Oh my night, Fatoum!
If I had to meet you and cross the sea,
I would build a bridge,
And if you were in the sky,
I would set a ladder!
For you, I went to Algiers,
For you, I would go to Rome.

***

Dieu est mon ami et donne au cœur ce qu'il désire.
Oh, combien le cœur s'appelle son ami!
Dieu, rendez l'âme à son corps après sa torture,
Et rendez l'oiseau à sa cage après sa fuite,
Et rendez, même de très loin,
Les absents à leurs aimées!

***

Ô toi, maîtresse de ce jardin, pourquoi es-tu fâchée?
As-tu peur que je me promène chez toi?
Ne crains rien, je n'entrerai pas, je suis lasse.
Je ne mangerai pas tes fruits, je n'ai pas faim.
Mais pour ton mari, méfie-toi,
Je te le prendrai!

***

Ô toi qui marches à l'aube,
Maîtresse aux babouches et aux longs cheveux moites!
Ton visage est semblable à la ronde lune
Et ton nom est aussi gracile que la fleur: Sissan.
Maudit soit celui qui dira
Que cette beauté est une négresse!

***

God is my friend and gives to the heart what it desires
Oh, how the heart calls to its lover!
God, give the soul back to the body after its torture,
And give the bird to its cage after its flight,
And give back, even from very far away
Those who are absent to their beloveds!

***

Oh you, mistress of this garden, why are you angry?
Are you afraid I'll walk where you live?
Fear nothing, I won't come in, I'm weary.
I won't eat your fruits, I'm not hungry.
But as for your husband, watch out,
I'll take him!

***

Oh you who walk at dawn,
Mistress in slippers and with long moist hair!
Your face is like the round moon
And your name is as slender as a flower: Sissan.
Cursed be he who will say
That this beauty is a negress!

***

Je suis descendue au fond de la mer
Et j'ai mis le sable bouillant dans les plis de ma robe.
La mer m'a dit que Dieu me rendrait le bonheur,
Que Dieu arrange tout.
Je suis descendue dans le jardin,
J'ai mis une petite voilette de jasmin
Et un grand voile d'œillets.
Jeunes filles, je vous donne un conseil:
Ne vous mariez pas avec des marins.
Ils gonflent avec le vent les voiles de leur navire
Et vous laissent un ruisseau de larmes sur les joues.
Je vous donne un conseil, jeunes fille:
Ne vous mariez pas avec des marins.

***

Je suis montée à la terrasse et j'ai déroulé un tapis.
Des oiseaux aux plumes rouges sont descendus.
Je leur ai demandé comment est la vie?
Ils m'ont répondu: paisible et heureuse.
Et toutes les richesses de Tunis seront tiennes.

***

Joue et ris! Les malheurs sont ta route.
Les jours prochains seront peut-être meilleurs.
Dieu aura pitié de nous
Et nous serons comme des étagères élevées.

***

I went down to the bottom of the sea
And I put boiling sand in the folds of my dress.
The sea said to me that God would make me happy,
That God takes care of everything.
I went down into the garden,
I placed a little veil of jasmine
And a big spray of carnations.
Young girls, I'll give you some advice:
Don't marry sailors.
They swell the sails of their ships with wind
And leave you with a stream of tears on your cheeks.
I'll give you some advice, young girls:
Don't marry sailors.

***

I went up onto the terrace and I unrolled a carpet.
Birds with red feathers came down.
I asked them how life was?
They replied: peaceful and happy.
And all the riches of Tunis will be yours.

***

Play and laugh! Misfortune is your path.
Perhaps the days to come will be better.
God will have pity on us
And we will be like high floors.

The Poets

Nouredine Aba (1921-96)
Born in Sétif, Algeria, he worked as a journalist, and reported on the Nurmeberg trials. His books include *La Toussaint des énigmes* and *Gazelle après minuit*.

Bachir Hadj Ali (1920-1989)
Born in the Algiers casbah, he was the general scretary of the Algerian Communist Party. He took part in the war of liberation, but after independence he was arrested and tortured. His books include *Chants pour les nuits de septembre, Que la joie demeure* and *Soleils sonores.*

Mohamed Belkacem Amar
Born in 1931 in Biskra, Algeria he studied psychology at the University of Damas. He took part in the committee for independence during the revolution, and was subsequently an advisor at the Algerian Ministry of Youth.

Djamal Amrani (1935-2005)
Born in Sour el-Ghozlane, Algeria he was a poet and journalist. During the war of liberation he was tortured in the Villa Susini by the paratroopers of General Massu. He knew Che Guevara and in 2004 received the Pablo Neruda medal for his poetry. His main publications were *Le Témoin, Déminer la mémoire* and *Œuvres choisies.*

Jean El-Mouhoub Amrouche (1907-1962)
Born in Petite Kabylie, Algeria, he lived in Tunis before settling in Paris. He founded the review *L'Arche* (in Algiers). His books include *Cendres, Etoile secrète* and *Mirages, Les cahiers de Barbarie.*

Aragon (1897-1982)
One of the key poets of the early Surrealist movement and later of the Resistance, he one of the intellectual leaders of the French

Communist Party. After the Second World War he was the director of *Lettres Françaises*. Among his many works are *Feu de joie, Le Crève-cœur, Les Yeux d'Elsa, Le Musée Grévin, Le Roman inachevé, Elsa, Les Poètes, Le Fou d'Elsa* and *Les Chambres*.

Mohamed Saleh Baouiya
Born in 1930 in Mariir, he studied medicine in Yugoslavia in 1962. He published a collection of poems in 1981.

Andrée Barret
Her books include *Progrès des signes sur l'esquisse, Des gens qui ne partaient jamais, Job, Jugement par le feu* and *L'Effort*.

Omar El Bernaoui (1935-2009)
Born in Biskra, he studied in Tunis and Baghdad and worked as a radio produce and announcer in Algeria.

Messaour Boulanouar
Born in 1938 in Sour el-Ghozlane, Algeria, he was imprisoned during the war of liberation. His books include *La meilleure force, Sous peine de mort, J'écris de Sour el-Ghozlane* and *Œuvres choisies*.

Yves Broussard
Born in 1937 in Marseille. In the early 1960s he was an editor of *Action poétique*. His books include *Nourrir le feu, Passant obstiné* and *Tenir parole*.

Gabriel Cousin (1918-2010)
Born in Droué in the Loire Valley, he was a poet and playwright. He published 35 books, including *La Vie ouvrière, L'Ordinaire amour* and *Dérober le feu*.

Maurice Cury
Born in 1932, he is a poet, novelist, screenwriter and essayist. His novel, *Sur la route de Salina* was filmed in 1970, starring Rita Hayworth. His many books include *La Forêt, Les Chevaux et les jardins, Les Pumas* and *La Jungle et le desert*.

Henri Deluy
Born in 1931 in Marseille. He edited *Action Poétique* fom 1955 to 2012, founded the international poetry biennale in Val-de-Marne, and has translated many writers from Dutch, German, Czech, Portuguese and Russian. Among his numerous collections are *L'Infraction*, *Premières suites*, *L'heure dite* and *L'Imprévisible passé*.

Mohammed Dib (1920-2003)
Born in Tlemcen, Algeria. He was a primary school teacher, a journalist, novelist and poet. He won the Grand Priz de la francophonie in 1994. Amongst his books are *Ombre gardienne* and *Feu, beau feu*.

Charles Dobzynski
Born in 1929 in Warsaw, he has lived in France since 1930. A journalist, critic, poet and translator, he was for many years editor in chief of the review *Europe*. He is a member of the Mallarmé Academy, president of the jury for the Apollinaire prize. His many books of poetry include *La vie est un orchestra*, *Corps à réinventer*, *J'ai failli la perdre* and *Le Baladin de Paris*. In 2012 he was awarded the Grand Prix de Poésie de la Société des Gens de Lettres.

Jacques Dubois
Born in 1928. He worked for many years as a photo-journalist and journalist. During the Algerian War he was a reserve officer until he went AWOL. Today, he cultivates his garden.

Jacques Gacheron (1920-2009)
Born in Beauce. He was one of the young poets of the Resistance, and a colleague of Eluard and Tzara. After the Second World War he taught philosophy and art, and worked for *La Nouvelle Critique* and the review *Europe*. His major works included the opera *Les Canuts* (with music by Joseph Kosma), *Le Chahier grec*, *La maison du sourd*, *Entre mon ombre et la lumière* and *Etat de veille*.

Georges-Louis Godeau (1921-1999)
From 1943 to 1981 he worked as a civil engineer. His poetry was translated into several languages, including Japanese, Russian and German. He received the Max-Pol Fouchet prize. His books include *Les mots difficiles*, *Votre vie m'intéresse* and *Après tout*.

Anna Gréki (1931-1996)
Born in Batna, Algeria. She was imprisoned during the war of liberation. Her collections include *Algérie, capitale Alger* and *Temps fort*.

Alain Guérin
Born in 1932 in the Dordogne. A historian of the Resistance, he was a journalist at *L'Humanité* and secretary of the Young Poets group gathered around Elsa Troilet in the 1950s. He has published several collections of poetry, including *Complot, Cosmos Brasero, Les Dits du Meunier* and *L'Ange et l'espion*. In 2003 he was awarded the Prix Verlaine de l'Académie Française.

Joseph Julien Guglielmi
Born in 1929 in Italy. He was a member of the editorial committee of *Action Poétique*. He has published several collections of poetry, essays and translations, especially of American poets. Among his books are *Ville ouverte*, *L'Eveil*, *Aube*, *Late* and *Fins de vers*.

Guillevic (1907-1997)
Born in Carnac in Brittany. A professisonal economist, he published more than forty collections of poetry, including *Terraqué, Terre à bonheur, Encoches, Art poétique, Relier* and *Vivre en poésie*.

Malek Haddad (1927-1978)
Born in Constantine. In 1974 he was elected secretary of the Union of Algerian Writers. Amongst his publications are *Le malheur en danger Je t'offrirai une gazelle* and *Les Zéros tournent mal*.

Kateb Yacine (1929-1989)
Born in Constantine. He took part in the demonstrations of 8 May 1945, when he was still a schoolboy in Sétif. A poet, novelist, playwright and journalist, he directed the regional Theatre of Sidi Bel Abbès. His many books include *Nedjma, Soliloques, le Polygone étoilé* and *Mohamed, prends ta valise.*

Henri Kréa (1933-2000)
Born in Algiers. He was a playwright, journalist, novelist and poet. His many books include *Longue durée, La révolution et la poésie sont une seule et même chose* and *Tombeau de Jugurtha.*

Alain Lance
Born in 1939 near Rouen. He has translated many German writers into French. From 1995 to 2004 he was director of the French Writers' Centre. Among his collections are *Distrait du désastre, Temps criblé, le Temps qu'il fait, Brefs du vingtième Quatrains pour Esteban* and *Divers avant l'hiver.*

André Liberati
Born in 1927 in Beirut. He was an associate of Benjamin Péret and André Breton. His many books include *Vieux capitaine, Le Cœur secret, La mort amoureuse, La transparence des pierres, Nadir* and *L'Exaltation de la Sainte Croix.*

Bernard Mazo (1939-2012)
Born in Paris. His many books of poetry include *Dans l'insomnie de la mémoire, La cendre des jours, Cette absence infinie, La vie foudroyée* and an essay *Sur les sentiers de la poésie.*

Henri Meschonnic (1932-2009)
Born in Paris. A poet, linguist, essayist and translator, he published over sixty books, including *Dédicaces Proverbes.* He was awarded the Max Jacob Prize and the Mallarmé Prize.

Jean Pélélgri (1920-2003)
Born in 1920 in Rovigo, Algeria. He was a novelist, poet, playwright and teacher. His books included *Les oliviers de justice,*

Le Maboul, Les monuments du deluge, le cheval dans la ville and *Les étés perdus.*

Jean Pérol
Born in 1932 in Vienne, Isère. A poet and novelist, he was director of the Institute Franciais in Japan from 1984 to 1989. His books include *Sang et raisons d'une presence, A part et passager* and *Libre livre.*

Jean Perret
Born in 1924. For many years he ran a bookselling co-operative. He was part of the group of writers that included Georges Mounin, Gabriel Cousin, Jean Malrieu and Franck Venaille.

Madeleine Riffaud
Born in 1924. During the Second World War she joined the Resistance, was arrested, tortured and imprisoned. She reported on the French wars in Algeria and Vietnam for *L'Humanité*, and narrowly escaped an attempted assassination by the OAS. Her books of poery include *Le Poing Fermé, Le Cheval rouge* and *La folie du jasmine.*

Jean Sénac (1926-1973)
Born in Béni-Sat near Oran, he was assassinated in Algiers in 1973. An associate of Camus and René Char, he was a poet, essayist and radio broadcaster. Amongst his works are *Poèmes, Le Soleil sous les armes* and *Dérisions et vertiges.*

Pierre Seghers (1906-1987)
Born in Paris. He founded the Seghers publishing house in 1944 and later set up the City of Paris Poetry Centre. As a poet his main publications were *Le Cœur-Volant, Chansons et complaintes* and *Like a hand making a fist.*

Oliven Sten (1931-2006)
Born in Berlin, Armand Olivennes moved to France as a child refugee in 1937. He worked as a doctor and published several books of poetry, including *Le Passant démesuré, Circulaire à mon*

amoureuse, Du cœur sans gants aux gants sans cœur, L'enterreur and *Le Poème de l'homme machine.*

Annie Fiorio-Steiner
Born in 1928 in Marengo, Algeria. During the war of liberation she was part of the secret FLN network in Algiers until she was arrested and imprisoned for five years. After independence, she took up an important post in government administration.

Nourredine Tidafi (1929-1990)
Born in Marengo, Algeria. His books include *Sang du peuple* and *Le Toujours de la patrie.*

Lanza del Vasto (1901-1981)
Born in Italy, he studied in Paris, Florence and Pisa where he took his doctorate in philosophy. His books include *le Pèlerinage aux sources,* about meeting Gandhi.

Franck Venaille
Born in 1936 in Paris. He has published many books of poetry, including *Papiers d'identité, La Guerre d'Algérie, La Procession des pénitents, Hourra les morts Algeria* and *La Bataille des éperons d'or.*

Antoine Vitez (1930-1990)
Born in Paris. He worked as private secretary to Aragon and was later director of the Chaillot National Theatre, and deputy head of the Comédie-Francaise. He translated Chekhov, Mayakovsky, Sholokhov and Ritsos into French and published several collections of poetry.

Jean-Jacques Viton
Born in 1933. He was a member of the editorial board of *Action Poétique* in the early 1960s and then again in the 1990s, co-founder and member of the editorial board of *Manteia* (1967-1974) and co-founder of the International Assembly of Contemporary Poetry. He has published several books of poems, including *Kanaka, Je voulais m'en aller mais je n'ai pas bougé* and *Selected sueurs.*

Acknowledgements

'North Africa 1952' was first published in 1952 by Cercle d'Art, Paris with illustrations by Boris Taslitsky and Mireille Miailhe. 'Mohamed et Jean' recounts the events of 28 May 1952, the demonstration against the arrival of the American General Ridgway in Paris, the arrest of the writer André Stil, and the murder by the Parisian police of Belaïd Hocine. First published in *L'Humanité* in 1953. 'On les tue par le feu, l'eau, l'électricité' and 'Chanson pour Mouloud' were first published in *Cheval rouge* (1973). The poem by Aragon was first published in *Le roman inachevé* (1956). 'Pour la paix' was published in *Les Chevaux et les jardins* (1957). 'Paix en Algérie', 'Versailles, peut-être', 'Henry Alleg chez nous en France', 'Non-violence et vérité' and 'La gloire' were first published in *Action Poetique*. 'Visages' was first published in *Lettres françaises*. The poems in 'Homage to Maurice Audin' were first published as a pamphlet by *Action Poétique*. 'Celui qui donne au bien son âme' was first published in *Vieux capitaine* (1958). 'Chaque mort avait son visage' was first published in *Cantate aux inconnus* (1960). 'Pour voir clair' was first published in *Europe* 1962. 'Les paroles de la rose' was first published in *Les Lettres françaises*. 'Le droit de dire au monde' was first published in *Entretiens sur les Lettres et les Arts*. The poems on pp 112-163 were collected by the Algerian poets Amin Khan and Hamid Tibouchi. The poems on pp 116-171 were collected by the Algerian poet Amar Mérieche and translated from Arabic by Maram al-Masri. The Bwaqel songs on pp 178-185 were translated and adapted by Baya, Hamida Bouzelifa and Jean Sénac.